Sizing up Science

Which would you rather be told – that the human heart measures 15×9×9 cm, or that it is about the size of your fist? That the volume of an object is $50m^3$ or that it is as big as a double-decker bus? And did you know that if a man could jump proportionately as high as a flea he could leap over St Paul's Cathedral? These are just a sample of the many fascinating and often amusing analogies used in this book to render complicated scientific facts and figures comprehensible to the ordinary reader.

R. Houwink started his career as a chemical engineer and subsequently became director of a number of important institutions in the rubber and plastics industries. The author of many books, he has devoted his time since retirement to writing on the visualisation of science.

SIZING UP SCIENCE

R. Houwink

Beaver Books

First published in 1975 by
John Murray (Publishers) Limited,
50 Albemarle Street, London W1X 4BD

This paperback edition published in 1977 by
The Hamlyn Publishing Group Limited
London · New York · Sydney · Toronto
Astronaut House, Feltham, Middlesex, England

ISBN 0 600 38211 7

Printed in England by
Cox & Wyman Limited,
London, Reading and Fakenham
Set in Monotype Baskerville

Contents

Preface

The purpose of this book

This book represents an endeavour to select and present some examples of striking, even surprising, numerical relationships from the almost unlimited store of scientific data. The reader will find here a collection of 'fixed points', an aid – so it is hoped – to understanding the much greater mass of data which will be found in text-books on the subjects dealt with. Such fixed points can become mental 'images', more readily retained than the exact, useful, but sometimes exceedingly dry series of numbers and symbols to be found in such text-books. A vivid image may not only be surprising in itself but, as the author knows from his own experience, also evocative of other, sometimes quite unexpected, ideas.

Unfortunately many scientists, even teachers and authors whose task it is to translate scientific findings into a generally comprehensible form, are still so under the influence of mathematical formulae and procedures that they forget to pass on to others the real meaning of their numerical data and results. I hope that this book will help them to comprehend and to appreciate more the deeper significance of scientific data so that they can explain them to others by means of *visualisation.*

The book does not strive at completeness: the treatment of any one subject is restricted to a few selected examples which may induce the reader to apply such ideas to his own particular field.

Acknowledgements

In the first place sincere thanks are due to J. Jackson whose advice during the translation contributed considerably to the conception of this book. Later on L. R. Middleton took over this task and also made many valuable comments which led to great improvements. A special word of thanks is due to the late M. Vertregt, with whom the author was in constant contact

concerning mathematical and other scientific questions: his spirit lives on throughout the book.
Some of the sections were written in collaboration with, or modified as a result of suggestions made by, the following colleagues: R. W. de Decker (Noise pollution), F. V. B. Dumoulin and B. J. G. van der Pot (Our motor, the heart), E. H. Houwink (Man and his relatives), B. Houwink (Dental caries), J. Jackson (Digging the world's canals), and M. Vertregt (Nature's energy; Holding our neighbours fast; Creation; Saving Apollo 12 from burn-up).

1 Why size up science, and how can we do it?

What do huge numbers convey to us?

Let us imagine that a conference is being held on the subject 'Just Numbers' and that the chairman is the eminent mathematical scientist Professor Gratensmall. He begins by pointing out the enormous range of sizes and numbers which every scientist encounters in his studies, and the difficulty of passing this kind of information on to others in such a way that it is not dismissed as mere jargon. As numbers become larger, this problem becomes more and more difficult. How does he make clear the significance of

a distance of 100,000 kilometres
one light year, ten million million (10^{13}) kilometres
a speed of one million (10^6) kilometres per hour
an area of 1000 square kilometres
a volume of 1000 cubic kilometres
the Earth's age, nearly five thousand million (5×10^9) years?

Very small numbers can be just as difficult to grasp:

one micron, one ten-thousandth (10^{-4}) of a centimetre
one nanosecond, one thousand-millionth (10^{-9}) of a second
one picosecond, one million-millionth (10^{-12}) of a second
the lifetime of some nuclear particles, 10^{-23} seconds.

How to visualise data[1]

Two very important elements in the dissemination of the results

[1]For references see Bibliography, page 135.

of scientific studies are (a) the selection of a generally applicable system for expressing measured quantities in numerical terms, and (b) the visualisation of these quantities.

It is helpful not only to use the new (metric) *Système Internationale* ('SI') but also to choose quantities or units whose sizes can be readily grasped. A medical text-book might state that impulses traverse the human nervous system at 1000 millimetres per second, but a more recognisable expression for this speed is 3½ kilometres per hour (2 m.p.h.) – the right pace for an evening stroll.

However, specialists have a right to their own 'jargon' – even if it is meaningless to the rest of the world. A good example is the aircraft designers' *mach* – the speed of sound in air (340 metres per second at 15 °C) – which is very important in certain aspects of aircraft operation, for when the speed exceeds 1 mach people on the ground hear the well-known 'sonic boom'. But the layman would probably prefer to be told that this speed is 1220 kilometres per hour (760 m.p.h.), ten times the speed he might reach when driving fast on a motorway.

Very large or very small quantities can often be related to real objects, giving us a better idea of the sizes involved; in the following range of volumes, the vital point is to choose the appropriate order of magnitude:

50 m^3	A 70-seater motor bus
100 m^3	A spacious room
1000 m^3	A medium-sized house
10,000 m^3	A village church
100,000 m^3	A modern oil-tanker

Writers of scientific text-books often miss opportunities of relating numerical data to everyday objects. They might say, for instance, that at room temperature one cubic metre of air contains 17 grams of water vapour at saturation point; but how many would go further and point out that the ratio of the volume of liquefied water to air at saturation point is the same as that of the tip of one's little finger (1·2 cubic centimetres) to one's whole body (70 litres for an average adult)?

An electronics expert may find that the purity requirements for one of the materials used in making transistors allows only one 'foreign' atom for every 200 million atoms of the substance itself. But his less expert friends will be better served by the information that this degree of purity is something like 'just one foreigner in the whole of the USA'.

Population densities are usually expressed as a number per unit of area, for example, twenty-five people per square kilometre (sixty-five per square mile) of the Earth's whole land area. A vivid illustration of the meaning of this figure is that the average area occupied by each man would be something like Grosvenor Square, London, or Union Square, New York, both about 40,000 square metres (48,000 square yards) in area.

At this stage the professor takes the opportunity to stress a point which seems trivial but which is nevertheless important in visualising data. We may feel that we have just expressed the 40,000 square metres per human being in an adequate way by means of the well-known squares in London and New York. But how many people actually know these squares and can form a clear image of them in their minds?

On the other hand, most people have a good idea of the size of a football pitch – 7200 square metres (9000 square yards). Thus the area per person could be said to equal five football pitches. Of course, not all football grounds are the same size so this statement cannot be exact; but it is the author's aim to present concepts that are simple to visualise and throughout this book there will be approximations when they are likely to be helpful to the reader.

Limits to the art of visualising data

Experience has shown that quite extensive trials are often needed before we find a picture that relates intelligibly to extremes of data. Let us take as an example the visualisation of 10^{22}, a figure which happens to express some remarkable relationships. Consider this:

The volume of a (small) virus is to that of a man as the volume of the man is to that of the Earth – a ration of 1 to 10^{22}.

The figure 10^{22} also expresses:

The number of planets, stars and other heavenly bodies in the observable universe.
The number of molecules in a drop of water the size of a pea (one-third of a cubic centimetre).
The number of cubic centimetres in the Arctic Ocean, or twice the number in the Mediterranean Sea.

(By the way, the number of human red blood-corpuscles on Earth is estimated at 10^{22}.)

Three possible ways of visualising this impressive number 10^{22} illustrate the drastic effects caused by a change in the arithmetic and in the units chosen for the comparison:

A grain of sand, conveniently cubical with a side of 0·1 millimetre, is perhaps the smallest object that we can easily see. 10^{22} times the *length* of its side is 10^{15} kilometres (6×10^{14} miles) nearly seven million times the distance from the Earth to the Sun, an *astronomical* distance quite beyond our capacity to visualise.

10^{22} times the area of one *face* of the tiny cube (i.e. 0·01 square millimetre) amounts to 100 million (10^8) square kilometres, easily ten times the area of the USA. It is still difficult to imagine such an enormous area, but it does at least give us some idea of the vast scale involved.

Finally, 10^{22} times the *volume* of our sand grain (i.e. 0·001 cubic millimetre) is only ten cubic kilometres, the volume of a cube 2·15 kilometres each way. We can readily visualise this standing in London with its base occupying an area about $1\frac{1}{2}$ times that of Regent's Park. In New York City it would take up a substantial part of Lower Manhattan, an area bounded by the Hudson River, 22nd Street, Madison Avenue and 59th Street. As to height (at 2150 metres, about 7000 feet) our cube would equal some of Norway's higher peaks or, in the USA, the Black Hills of South Dakota. In the shape of a pointed mountain with the same base, it would reach a height of 6500 metres (21,000 feet), about twice that of Mount Etna in Sicily and very nearly as tall as Mount McKinley in Alaska. Instead of places in London or New York we can again use football pitches, tennis courts and other familiar areas. Let the reader try it for himself.

Any number between 1 and 10^{22} can be visualised in a similar way, either starting with an object larger than the 0·1 cubic millimetre grain of sand, or finishing with something smaller than the 2·15 cubic kilometre mountain 6500 metres high.

To show what this kind of thing can lead to, Professor Gratensmall suggests that we try to visualise the much smaller number 10^9 (1000 million), a figure that is often mentioned in books: for instance, in 1825 there were about 10^9 people living on Earth. This time each grain of sand represents a human being. But since the side of a grain of 0·1 millimetre is only just visible to the naked eye, the professor uses one-millimetre and one-centimetre grains, sizes more familiar to laymen. As expected, with the much smaller figure of 10^9, simpler pictures come into existence.

Table 1. Visualising 10^9 using grains of sand with a side of one millimetre and one centimetre, respectively.

	One-millimetre grain	*One-centimetre grain*
Length of grain enlarged 10^9 times	1000 kilometres	10,000 kilometres
	= distance from London to Prague, or New York to Chicago	= distance from North Pole to Equator
Surface area of grain enlarged to 10^9 times	1000 square metres	100,000 square metres
	= 32 × 32 metres	= 320 × 320 metres
	= 4 tennis courts	= Buckingham Palace Gardens, or Washington Square, New York.
Volume of grain enlarged 10^9 times	1000 litres	1,000,000 litres
	= volume of two horses	= 10^3 cubic metres
		= a medium-sized house

Comparing these two sizes, Professor Gratensmall prefers the one-millimetre grain in spite of the fact that one centimetre is a more familiar quantity, because the pictures obtained with the 1-mm grain are so much simpler to visualise. For instance, the distance from London to Prague (or from New York to Chicago) will mean more to most of us than the distance from the North Pole to the Equator. Other people, however, might choose the 1-cm grain: it is up to you.

Before he closes the conference Professor Gratensmall wants to know how the members of the audience would prefer to visualise the size of a human heart. Would they be happy to think of it as being the size of a box measuring 15 cm × 9 cm × 9 cm, or would they rather know that a person's heart and his fist were about the same size? 'And,' he says, 'I suggest that for homework you try to visualise the figure 10^{80}, which is thought to be the number of particles in the observable universe. I hope that at least one of you will have a sensible answer for me tomorrow, but I doubt it.'

2 Nature's building blocks

Atoms

The Ancient Greeks thought that if they split matter further and further, they would eventually arrive at something which is *a-tomos* (un-splittable). Many scientists used to be doubtful whether we would ever be able to see this 'smallest unity' of matter, but we have now reached a stage where we can see individual atoms as light spots by means of a field electron microscope. Our next ambition is to 'see' the internal structure of the atom, and the picture presented below may give an idea of what many scientists hope one day to see.

Consider a carbon atom, the backbone of organic chemistry – the means of life. Its nucleus consists of twelve particles altogether, six positively-charged protons and six uncharged neutrons. Around this nucleus spin six negative electrons, two in inner orbits and four – the valency electrons – in outer orbits. Although it is rather speculative to give any of these particles a definite 'diameter', let us say that the carbon nucleus as a whole has a diameter of 6×10^{-13} centimetres.*

Scaling this nucleus up $1{\cdot}7 \times 10^{12}$ times, we see a marble about half an inch (one centimetre) in diameter. If we put this – instead of the usual football – in the centre of a stadium which, with a diameter of 260 metres (290 yards) represents the scaled-up atom, the outer (valency) electrons would move in different planes around the heads of the spectators at the back of the stands, 130 metres (145 yards) from the marble. The two inner electrons would rotate in a similar way 15 metres (16 yards) from the marble. One of the older spectators, a man trained in classical

*The so-called 'classical diameter' of an electron has been calculated from its rest mass.

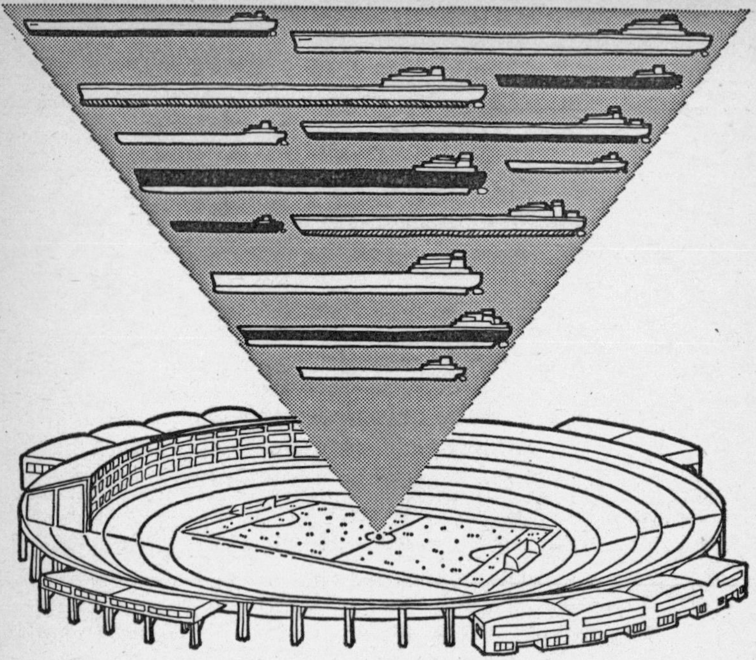

Figure 1. Instead of a football, at the centre of this stadium there is a marble made of one cubic centimetre of nuclear material, which means that it has a mass exceeding 10^8 tonnes – the capacity of 500 super-tankers. Can the stadium support the weight of this marble?

physics, looking around this remarkable empty stadium, had expected to see the electrons as real globules but a young physicist explains that he is unlikely to see them for two reasons:

(a) An electron is nowadays thought of as not so much an object as a 'probability zone' enveloping the nucleus by a sort of hollow spherical 'mesh' of energy.

(b) The speed of an electron in its orbit is, depending on its sort, something like 7000 times that of a modern jet passing overhead at 1500 kilometres per hour, so that it would disappear before our classical physicist could see it.

At the entrance to the stadium is a poster with the following information:

Table 2. Basic data concerning the constituents of an atom

	Mass (g)	*Classic diameter* (cm)	*Density* (g/cm^3)
electron	$9{\cdot}1 \times 10^{-28}$	$2{\cdot}2 \times 10^{-14}$	around
proton or neutron	$1{\cdot}7 \times 10^{-24}$	$2{\cdot}6 \times 10^{-13}$	$1{\cdot}75 \times 10^{14}$*
nucleus of a C atom (6 protons + 6 neutrons)	$2{\cdot}2 \times 10^{-23}$	$6{\cdot}0 \times 10^{-13}$	

According to this the diameter of a proton would be something like twelve times that of an electron and its density is thought to be of the same order, about $1{\cdot}75 \times 10^{14}$ grams per cubic centimetre. This density, almost beyond our conception, is so fantastic that our little nuclear marble would have a mass exceeding 10^8 tonnes – the load capacity of some 500 super-tankers each carrying 200,000 tonnes. Placed in the stadium, the marble would sink straight through the Earth's crust. If the marble was 1½ times the size of the stadium, its mass would be equal to that of the whole Earth.

Another feature is that more than 99·97 per cent of the mass of the atom is lodged within its nucleus: in one cubic centimetre of nuclear material – if we could make it – there would be 10^{38} nucleons†. A colossal number like this completely overshadows the 3×10^{22} molecules present in a cubic centimetre of water, which was quoted on page 16 as an example of extreme numbers occurring in science; 10^{38} water molecules would occupy three cubic kilometres (0·8 cubic mile), which is 20,000 times the volume of one of the highest sky-scrapers in New York, the Empire State Building.

The analogy of a marble in a stadium can be used for any of the 105 known atoms and the two extreme cases would be:

For the lightest element, hydrogen, the marble would be

*According to present theories the density of an electron is $1{\cdot}63 \times 10^{14}$ g per cc, that of a proton or neutron $1{\cdot}85 \times 10^{14}$ g per cc.

†Nucleons are the protons and neutrons in the nucleus of an atom.

0·4 centimetre in diameter, placed in a stadium 170 metres (200 yards) across.

For the heaviest element, uranium, there would have to be a marble of diameter 2·7 centimetres in the centre of a stadium 500 metres (550 yards) wide.

Molecules

The simplest molecules consist of only two or three atoms and we can clearly use the same comparison for these that we used for atoms themselves – although we would have to imagine several stadia linked together. But we shall have to find other ways of describing the complicated macromolecules which are found in the 200,000 sorts of plants and the 1,000,000 sorts of animals known to us, as well as in plastics, fibres and rubbers. Here is an example of the kind of problem we shall encounter:

A rubber macromolecule with a polymerisation degree of 3000 has as its backbone a chain of 15,000 carbon atoms. Stretched out on our enlarged scale, the chain of 15,000 stadia would almost reach from London to Mecca, or from New York to Los Angeles (about 4000 kilometres or 2500 miles).

It would look like a hollow tube, with walls formed by a 'mesh' of energy, the rotating electrons. Its width would be comparable to that of the Rhine in Germany (260 metres); the nuclei, 260 metres apart, would each have a mass equal to the load carried by 500 super-tankers. A molecule of DNA* – one of the longest known – if straightened out would stretch twice this distance, from London to Calcutta or from New York to Rio de Janeiro.

Restless silver atoms[2]

Although a silver spoon might, to all appearances, be lying quietly on the table as we enjoy our meal, its constituent atoms are not only in constant vibration but are also playing a sort of

*Deoxyribonucleic acid, very important in the life and reproduction of cells.

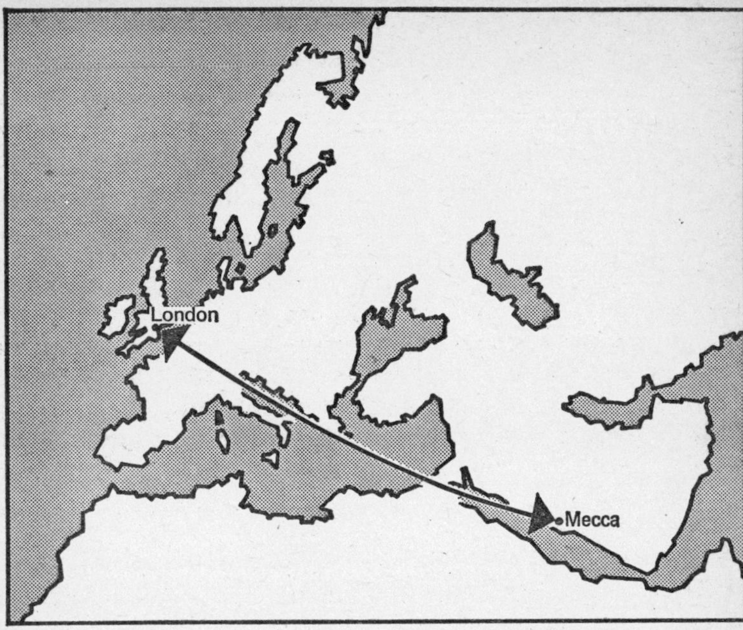

Figure 2. If the carbon nuclei of a rubber macromolecule were enlarged to the size of marbles (an enlargement of $1{\cdot}7 \times 10^{12}$ times, so that the nuclei measure one centimetre across), the whole molecule would reach from London to Mecca.

'musical chairs' as a result of thermal agitation. This happens even at normal room temperature, which is far below the melting point of the metal (960 °C).

However, for any particular atom such a movement is a very rare event, so rare that only now might we expect to see a second shift by an atom which last made a move when birds began to appear on the Earth, 100 million years ago. Throughout this period, our atom has been in constant vibration at $4{\cdot}6 \times 10^{12}$ times per second, and has therefore had this number of opportunities to change its place every second; this is as if all the present inhabitants of the Earth had, in the same second, well over 1000 chances of making a move.

So the truth of the saying attributed to Heraclitos, who lived in Ancient Greece around 500 BC, seems rather doubtful:

panta rei, oeden menei (all is flowing, nothing is fixed).

On the other hand, in each cubic centimetre of silver there are 6×10^{22} atoms and, of these, calculation shows that a number like the present population of Canada (more than 20 million) change their places in every second. From *this* point of view *panta rei* – all is flowing – seems a little more accurate.

The melting point of silver is 960 °C, and if a silver object (not, hopefully, one of the best spoons) is heated up, the frequency with which a particular atom is displaced increases very rapidly to values which can be represented thus:

At 370 °C the atom moves at the rate of the average human heart-beat, just over once per second.

At 375 °C its movements resemble the quiet flight of a stork, whose wings beat at $1\frac{1}{2}$ to 2 strokes per second.

At 400 °C it reaches the rate of the separate strokes of a skilled typist, just distinguishable as she does three to four letters each second.

At 425 °C the activity is that of a virtuoso pianist who could perform Chopin's 'Minute Waltz' at the record speed of 20 notes per second.

At 500 °C it moves ten times as fast as before – as fast as the wings of a fly buzzing about, which we see only as a blur and hear as a musical note.

The Greek saying *panta rei* is now completely justified, even though we are still 460 °C below the temperature at which silver becomes visibly a liquid, i.e. its melting point.

Knocking at the doors of freedom

Let us take a small cubical container, one centimetre along each edge, and fill it with air (or any other stable gas) under normal atmospheric conditions.

Such is the activity of the molecules of the air (or gas)[2], even under these mild everyday conditions, that on each inner face of the cube (of area one square centimetre) there will be 3×10^{23} 'knocks' per second from molecules moving at a speed equivalent to that of a modern jet aircraft (1500 kilometres per hour or 930 m.p.h.).

For the human race to match this number of knocks, everyone who has ever lived – perhaps 10^{11} people altogether – would have had to be busy knocking once per second for the last 100,000 years – since the time of Neanderthal Man – and we would have had to bang our fists very quickly to reach the 'jet' speed of the molecules, some 410 metres per second.

A fuse blows

We are in a house wired for electricity with a safety fuse which will blow at a loading of six amperes. Now in order to visualise the $3{\cdot}6 \times 10^{19}$ electrons which must flow through the circuit to blow the fuse, let us imagine a vast bathing beach on the east coast of America, stretching from the northernmost point of Labrador to the southernmost point of Florida – as long as the total coastline encircling the British Isles (7000 kilometres or 4300 miles)*. If this gigantic beach were 50 metres (60 yards) wide and 10 metres (11 yards) deep, and if we could change all its grains of sand into electrons† then all these electrons entering the house in one second through the electric mains would produce an electric current of six amps and the fuse would 'blow' (see Figure 3 overleaf).

The lives of nuclear particles

Protons, liberated from atoms, are stable for periods of over 10^{28} years but for liberated neutrons this figure is only 15 minutes. Other nuclear particles decay within minute fractions of a

*Because of the irregularities of these coastlines the estimated figures are larger than the simplified coastlines mentioned in some encyclopedias.
† One cubic millimetre is supposed to contain about ten fine particles.

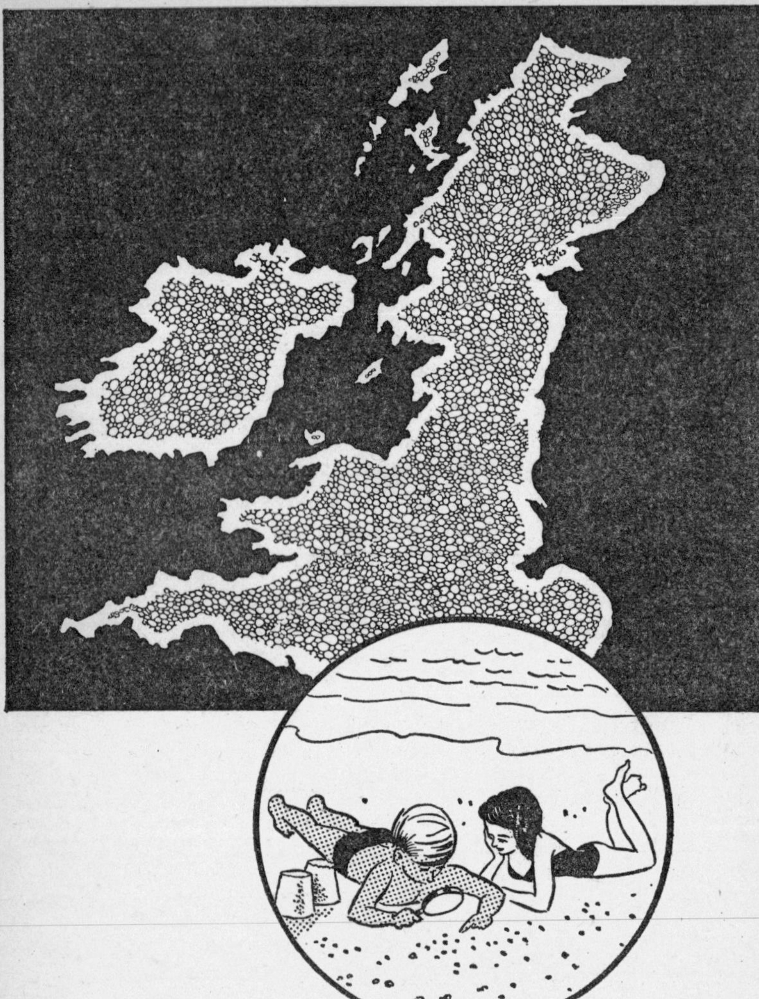

Figure 3. If we could change into electrons all the $3{\cdot}6 \times 10^{19}$ grains of sand in this gigantic beach 50 metres wide and 10 metres deep (55 yards $\times$ 11 yards) which surrounds the British Isles, and then cause all these electrons to flow into a house in one second . . . a six-amp fuse would **blow!**

second. If the lifespan of a neutron is the time you might take to drink a pint of beer, you would have to be at the bar for 20 million million times the lifetime of the universe in order to follow the proton's course of life. The life span of some particles is of the order of 10^{-23} seconds, so we would see alternate births and deaths of these particles at least as many times in one second as the number of heavenly bodies in the observable universe (10^{22}).

High temperatures

Collisions between high-energy nuclear particles produce, under suitable experimental conditions, local temperatures thought to be of the order of one million million (10^{12}) degrees Celsius[3]. How do these compare with more familiar temperatures? Consider an oven capable of heating its contents at the rate of 1 °C per second:

Soon after 1½ minutes, water would begin to boil.

After 25 minutes, iron would melt (1500 °C).

After 100 minutes, the temperature would be that of the Sun's surface (6000 °C).

Only after 5½ *months* would the temperature reach that of the Sun's interior, estimated at 14,000,000 °C.

After 1¼ *years*, it would equal the highest experimental temperature ever reported on actual matter, 40,000,000 °C, which we may call our highest 'effective' temperature.

After 11 years, it would be 350,000,000 °C, the temperature in a thermo-nuclear explosion.

Only after 31,000 years we would have reached the 10^{12} °C mentioned at the beginning, which is believed to be developed constantly, if only *very* locally, in some experiments with high-energy particles.

After 58,000 years, the temperature would be $1{\cdot}86 \times 10^{12}$ °C. This is the level believed to be reached if the collision energy is forced to its maximum. Perhaps this temperature, 120,000 times that of the Sun's interior, is the highest attained not only on or in our Earth, but in the whole Universe.

Breaking the sound-barrier noiselessly

Extremely small smoke particles can, with the help of a good microscope, be seen to be 'pushed around' by the rapid motion of the molecules of the air in which they are suspended. These molecular movements are along short straight paths, constantly interrupted by collisions with other molecules.

But if a carbon dioxide molecule could be given an undeflected run along the Equator, it would travel around the world in just over 24 hours; its speed, about 1500 kilometres per hour (940 m.p.h.), can be reached by many modern aircraft. A hydrogen molecule moves faster, and could complete the circular trip in six hours; its speed, 7000 kilometres per hour (4400 m.p.h.) may be equalled by commercial aircraft during the next few years.

Between collisions both these molecules move faster than sound (1225 kilometres per hour) yet we are not aware of any sonic booms. The explanation is that noise consists of pressure disturbances with many millions of molecules moving at the same time in the same direction, so individual molecules move in complete silence.

The cost of chemical analyses by computer

It is often possible nowadays to determine the arrangement of atoms within a complex molecule from various physical records – for example, from 'Gauss' functions. But for a molecule containing only ten atoms, 25 million integrals have to be worked out to test only one of several possible configurations.

A modern '$500 per hour' computer takes only one hour for this seemingly huge task (500 integrations for one cent), but it could easily be necessary to work out twenty different configurations before we could be certain which molecule we are dealing with. This may cost $10,000 in computer time, enough for eight delegates to travel by air (economy class) from New Zealand to a conference on 'Molecular Structure' in London, and back again – each journey, out and back, about half-way round the world.

3 This vast but little piece of earth

The size of the globe

On the vast scale of the Solar System, our globe is a very tiny object, only 13,000 kilometres (8000 miles) in diameter. However, on the human scale, a motorist prepared to drive 450 kilometres (280 miles) every day would need all of three months to complete a 'tour du Monde' if a road were built which encircled the Earth, and an energetic hiker would take three years if he walked 37 kilometres (23 miles) a day.

Temperature

If this road around the Earth passed through the Poles and also through one of the very hot desert regions, the travellers would encounter extremes of temperatures from −88 °C (−127 °F) up to +58 °C (+136 °F). This range, 146 °C (263 °F) is 32 times the tolerable limit of variation within the human body, which is from 36 °C (97 °F) to 40·5 °C (105 °F).

Wearing clothes is man's readiest way of keeping warm, and drinking plenty of liquid (mostly water) helps him to keep cool. On the average, humans acquire clothing at the rate of about 4 kilograms (9 lb) per year – twice the weight of liquid that most people drink *in a day* (about two litres).

The biosphere

This is the region of the Earth within which life is found. In the middle latitudes it extends up to 20 kilometres (66,000 feet) above sea-level, but at this upper limit a cubic metre of air contains only seven per cent of the number of molecules found in the same volume of air at sea-level; 95 per cent of all life is found in the limited zone from 0·1 kilometre below sea-level to some three kilometres above it.

A deep oil-well might reach far below the biosphere, but even at a depth of eight kilometres (26,200 feet) it would penetrate the Earth's diameter only in the ratio of one pace (0·6 metre, about two feet) to a walk of one kilometre (0·6 mile). Measurements taken down this well would show that the temperature rises two or three degrees Centigrade for every 100 metres of descent, so that a mine one kilometre (3300 feet) deep is intolerably hot unless it is well ventilated.

The deepest oceans reach depths of twelve kilometres but on a globe one metre in diameter they would only appear as small depressions, one millimetre deep. The highest mountain – Everest – would be represented by a hump 0·75 mm high and the biosphere at middle latitudes on this globe would be a layer 1·75 mm thick.

Water

Roughly two-thirds of the Earth's surface is covered by the salt water of the seas – indeed, the area of the Pacific Ocean alone is 25 per cent greater than the Earth's total land area. However, all the water on or near the Earth's surface, including snow and ice, (1,300,000,000 cubic kilometres, or $1{\cdot}3 \times 10^{18}$ tonnes), has only 1/5000 the mass of the Earth itself; and, incidentally, the mass of the atmosphere is only one-millionth that of the Earth. So, the ratio of the mass of water to the mass of Earth is that of a cup of tea (140 grams) to that of ten grown-up people (10×70 kilograms) and the air-to-earth ratio is that of one breath (0·7 gram) to that of the same ten people.

Here are some facts about the water over our globe:

If the Earth was flat its $1{\cdot}3 \times 10^{9}$ cubic kilometres of water would form a layer 2·5 kilometres deep over its whole surface.

Figure 4. The effect of throwing away a cupful of tea on the combined weight of these ten people is like removing all the water from the surface of the Earth. By the same comparison, a puff of breath represents the entire atmosphere.

The water of immediate use to man (i.e. excluding salt and frozen water) is only 1/100 of this: a layer 25 metres deep.

The water in vapour and liquid form in the atmosphere constitutes only 1/1000 of the 'usable water': a layer of 2·5 centimetres deep. This last quantity might seem small but it equals the contents of Lakes Huron and Michigan combined, 13,000 cubic kilometres.

Energy

We shall see on page 37 that the Earth receives a total of some $1{\cdot}21 \times 10^{14}$ kilowatts of 'useful' energy, enough to support one individual on every ten square metres of its surface (2·4 kW per person).

Us

World population has now exceeded 3700 million – which, incidentally, is roughly the number of years since the Earth's surface solidified. This will not remain true for long, however, because the world's population now grows each year by 100 million – the population of Japan.

A condensed calendar for the Earth[1]

The past

If the entire history of the Earth since its solidification 4700 million years ago is condensed into a single calendar year, one day of this year represents about ten million years of history.* On this time-scale, the gradual cooling of a certain cloud of hot gas through the liquid state to the externally-solid globe which we know as our Earth took nearly two 'condensed' years, corresponding to 6500 million years of actual time.

Here are some highlights from the last 3500 million years compressed to one year, and the clock has just finished chiming midnight on New Year's Eve, the last day of the year:

In May the first signs of life appeared – algae.

In early June, bacteria.

In the second week of December, vertebrates.

In the third week of December, mammals.

At about 6 p.m. on the 31st December came our primitive ancestor, 'Oldowan' man (who lived in the Olduvai Gorge in Africa two million years ago – see page 89).

During the last hour four separate Ice Ages occurred, the last of which (the Würm period) was most intense at about 13 minutes to 12. It ended only 1½ minutes ago (in reality 90,000 years ago).

At about 1 minute to 12, *Homo sapiens* began to scratch pictures on the walls of caves and during the course of this last minute the Egyptian pyramids have been built, the Dialogues of Plato have been written, and Jesus of Nazareth has lived and died.

*1 condensed calendar day – 10 million actual years (approximately).
1 condensed hour – 400,000 actual years (approximately).
1 condensed minute – 7000 actual years (approximately).
1 condensed second – 120 actual years (approximately).

As the clock struck the eighth chime of midnight, Columbus discovered America; 2½ seconds later George Washington died and Napoleon came to power.

During the last chime the steam engine changed the world, and in the last fraction of a second we have seen the beginning of the electronic revolution.

The future

Some forecasts as the next day begins:

Within a few tenths of a second (each tenth representing 12 real years) we can expect a manned experimental station on the moon, and perhaps a permanently orbiting space-laboratory.

Within five to ten minutes – about 50,000 real years – a new Ice Age, with no fossil fuels (coal and oil) to keep man warm, for these were exhausted in the first few seconds of the day. Atomic energy, the killer of hundreds of thousands in Japan just 0·2 second before the day began will still supply part of the energy man needs, although by then he may get his supplies directly from the Sun (see page 58).

But all these problems are as nothing compared with that of overcrowding; if present population trends continue, there will be hardly any standing-room on the Earth's surface within a few condensed seconds (see page 89).

The egg-shell we live on

In spite of its strength the shell of an egg is relatively thin – 0·3 millimetre, in fact – but how many people realise that the proportion of the thickness of the shell to the egg's overall size is roughly the same as the proportion of the thickness of the Earth's surface crust to the size of the whole Earth.

To reach the centre of the Earth we must first pass through 40 to 60 kilometres (24–37 miles) of this crust. After passing through some other solid zones we would reach the liquid core, 6350 kilometres (3960 miles) from the surface, the distance from Los Angeles or Baghdad to the North Pole.

It is remarkable that the whole volume of the Moon would furnish only 87 per cent of the material of the Earth's surface crust, taking 50 kilometres as its average thickness.

About 72 per cent of the Earth's surface lies deep below the sea and the remaining 28 per cent is mostly well above sea-level: the proportion of shallow sea and low-lying land is very small. The average depth of the sea is 3·8 kilometres (12,500 feet), the height of Granite Peak in the Absaroka range, Montana, or about three times the height of Ben Nevis. The deepest sounding taken so far is 12 kilometres (7 miles) at a point in the Western Pacific; this is almost 1⅓ times the height of Mount Everest (8848 metres, or 29,028 feet), which is itself – to descend into the Earth again – about the same as the world's deepest oil wells in Oklahoma. These deep drillings have penetrated only about 14 per cent of the surface crust – or 1/750 of the distance to the centre of the Earth. This is as if we had completed the first kilometre of a journey from our oil-well at Oklahoma City to St Louis, or from London to Inverness.

Apart from the sudden earth-movements which we experience as earthquakes, different parts of the Earth's crust are also moving slowly in relation to one another. The delicate measuring instruments in the observatories at Leipzig and Rome have revealed that these two locations have moved one finger's length closer to each other in the last 60 years, while the Heidelberg instruments show that the observatory there has moved a hand's length away from the North Pole in the course of the last 80 years. The Pharaohs would now find their pyramids four kilometres (2·5 miles) further southward than where they left them, and the American soldiers who landed in Europe during the Second World War (1945) had to sail nine metres (about ten yards) further than their predecessors 25 years earlier.

Still more remarkable, it has been found that the Earth's crust is sufficiently elastic to show measurable deformation under the weight of the water in some of the largest man-made lakes. Under large buildings the Earth inclines one-tenth of a millimetre towards the east in the morning and towards the west by the same amount in the evening, direct evidence of the Sun's gravitational attraction for a specific object on the Earth, as well as of the elasticity of the Earth's crust.

Sky-high life

Let us see what life is to be found on three high mountains:

The highest peak in the Alps, Mont Blanc, is 4810 metres (15,782 feet) high, the upper limit for green plant life in temperate latitudes.

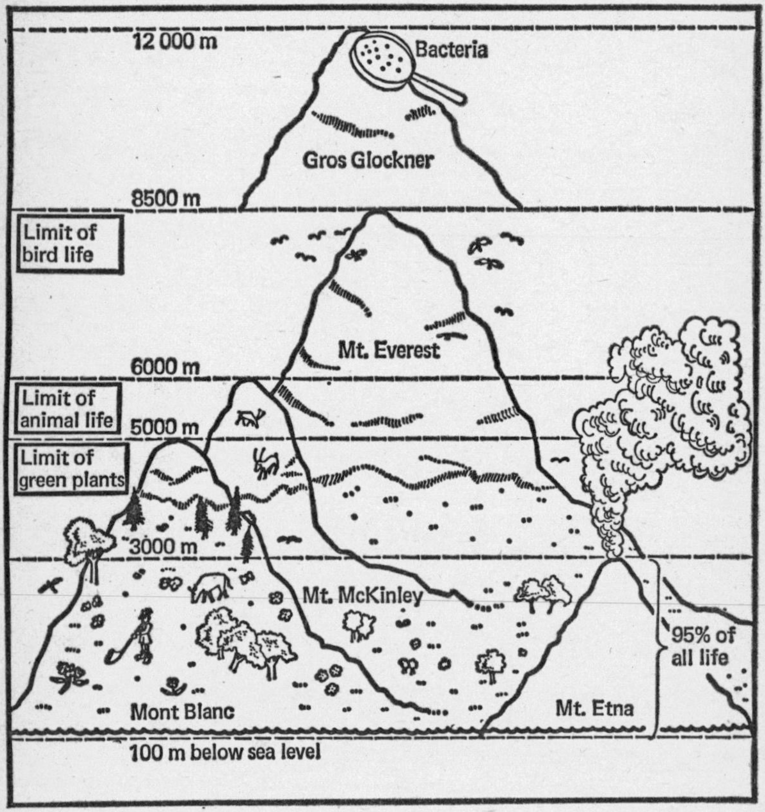

Figure 5. The limits of life.

The highest peak in North America, Mount McKinley in Alaska, is 6200 metres (20,300 feet) high, the upper limit for animal life.

The highest peak in the world, Mount Everest, is 8848 metres (29,028 feet) high, the approximate upper limit for the flight of birds.

Still higher, at about 12,000 metres (40,000 feet) – the height of another good-sized mountain above the top of Mount Everest – we would need a microscope to see the only forms of life there, bacteria and spores.

Ninety-five per cent of all life is lived in the region from 100 metres below sea level up to about 3000 metres above it, in all about the height of Mount Etna.

Take-off

The minimum vertical velocity needed to escape from the Earth's gravitational field is, at the surface of the Earth, and disregarding air-resistance, about 11 kilometres (7 miles) per second. So a motorist driving at 400 times his usual cruising speed (so fast that he could travel right round the Earth, 40,000 kilometres, in one hour) could, if he pointed his car straight up into the air, leave the Earth for ever.

Nature's energy[4, 5]

Our greatest source of power is the Sun, which supplies the Earth and its surrounding atmosphere with $1{\cdot}73 \times 10^{14}$ kilowatts ($1{\cdot}37 \times 10^{21}$ kilocalories per year)*. Thirty per cent of this stream is reflected back by the atmosphere as short-wavelength radiation; let us call the 70 per cent passing through the atmosphere 'useful energy' because in various ways it helps to make life possible. This power flux of $1{\cdot}21 \times 10^{14}$ kW ($9{\cdot}50 \times 10^{20}$ kcal per

*This influx is expressed in terms of the *solar constant*, which is defined as the mean rate of flow of solar energy across a unit of area perpendicular to the radiation and outside the atmosphere at the mean distance between the Earth and the Sun. This influx is $1{\cdot}97$ calories per square centimetre per minute which, integrated over the intercepting diametric plane of $1{\cdot}275 \times 10^{14}$ square metres adds up to $1{\cdot}73 \times 10^{14}$ kW or $1{\cdot}3 \times 10^{21}$ kcal per year.

year) is enough to supply 15,000 times our present food and power requirements (enough for 2·4 kW per person, see page 93), if it could be collected efficiently. Less well-known is the fact that a *neutrino* flux – presumably of the same power – reaches us, but happily most of it passes straight through the Earth. We make no use at all of another, even more powerful, energy source – the *rotation* of the Earth itself.

Here is a breakdown of the useful power that reaches the Earth from the Sun:

67 per cent of it is absorbed by the atmosphere, the land and the oceans and converted directly into heat at the ambient surface temperature; this portion would be sufficient for the food and power consumption of 10,000 times the Earth's population.

32 per cent is consumed in the hydrological cycle of evaporation and precipitation of water, and most of this too is eventually converted into heat. The energy involved is enough for about 5000 times the food and power consumption of mankind.

Of the 1 per cent that remains one-fifth produces effects which, although weak compared to the other quantities of energy that we have mentioned, are none the less spectacular to us. This fifth drives the atmospheric and oceanic convection currents, wind and waves, and is finally dissipated by friction into heat.

Finally an even smaller fraction – not even 0·03 per cent of the useful energy – amounting to 4×10^{10} kW (3×10^{17} kcal per year) is captured by leaves of plants, where it supplies the essential energy for photosynthesis. This amounts to five times the power used in human consumption. The efficiency of plants in converting the energy captured by all the plants on our globe into useful power is far below 20 per cent: man is for the most part living on stocks of 'fossil' fuels – coal, oil and gas – produced by energy from sunshine over the past 600 million years. It is alarming to think that our power requirements are doubling every ten years.

Power sources other than the Sun are the energy of the Earth's rotation, as we have mentioned, and the heat from its interior (volcanoes) – not forgetting the Moon, whose gravity produces the tides. Let us consider some of the most spectacular of these sources:

A form of energy without which most life is impossible is *rainfall*, part of the hydrological cycle. The continuous evaporation of water absorbs 29 per cent ($3{\cdot}5 \times 10^{13}$ kW) of the useful energy captured by the Earth. This might seem impressive, but the $4{\cdot}4 \times 10^5$ cubic kilometres of rain which falls down each year is not even 0·03 per cent of the contents of the Atlantic Ocean. Rain in its most spectacular form – a heavy cloudburst – can deposit more than an inch of water within 30 minutes: a depth of three centimetres has been recorded over an area of seven square kilometres (2·7 square miles) – about twice the area of the City of London. Altogether this amounts to 200,000 cubic metres of water, the volume of four million people falling on the heads of Londoners: each half hour over 2000 persons per second. To

Figure 6. A storm over London can contain enough energy to lift the whole population of China (800 million people) to the level of the highest peak in the Lake District (1000 metres).

form all the raindrops which make up this quantity from the atmosphere's water vapour, 540 kilocalories of latent heat of condensation must be abstracted from every kilogram of water condensed. So the energy used in the cloudburst would be in the region of 100,000 million (10^{11}) kcal. This would lift the whole population of China (approximately 800 million adults and children with an average mass of 50 kilograms) from sea-level to the height of the tallest peak in the Lake District (1000 metres, or 3200 feet).

The power of the wind is estimated at 2×10^{10} kW. This energy is difficult to exploit: if we could do it, we would have 2½ times as much as we would need for all our food and power. In its most concentrated form the wind can be a terrifying phenomenon – a *hurricane* – which could contain up to 3×10^{10} kW: that is 50 per cent more than the average power of all the winds blowing on the Earth at any given time. With power at this level, it is not surprising to hear of men being blown off the road by hurricane Alice or Zoë. Curiously enough, hurricanes are always identified by girls' names!

The movements of the seas and oceans – what we call *tides* – produce a rather low power-output estimated at 3×10^9 kW, not even half of our food-plus-power consumption. But it is enough to lift all the world's population to five kilometres (three miles) above sea-level once every hour. These tide movements are still hardly exploited, and neither are the thermal gradients in the oceans which might supply similar quantities of energy.

Flashes of lightning vary quite a lot in power. A modest flash might discharge 10^9 kW acting during 10^{-4} second and the total energy released in this tiny moment would be some 30 kilowatt hours*. This would lift 250 people to the top of our peak in the Lake District. But giant flashes have been recorded†, releasing enough energy for 6000 people to make the trip. Another source

*Figures in the literature vary between 10^8 and 10^{11} kilowatts with durations between 3×10^{-5} and 10^{-2} second, corresponding respectively to energy releases between 1 and 10^5 kilowatt hours.

†3×10^9 joules: *The Guinness Book of Records*, London 1972, page 63.

of energy that does not come from the Sun is that of *earthquakes.* The intensities of these disturbances are, like wind speeds, recorded on a scale where the highest number (12) means, for winds, a hurricane and, for earthquakes, a catastrophe. The highest readings recorded for earthquakes are 8 to 9 which have been measured on three occasions, the last one in 1960 in Chile, where the shocks lasted for some minutes. The energy of such an earthquake can reach up to $1{\cdot}5 \times 10^{11}$ kW h, equivalent to the food supply for the entire population of the world for a year.

Also independent of the Sun are the 3×10^{10} kW that come from our globe's interior, some of it through *hot-springs* and *volcanoes*, but together these contribute only a hundredth of the total amount. Such contributions might seem negligible, but it may

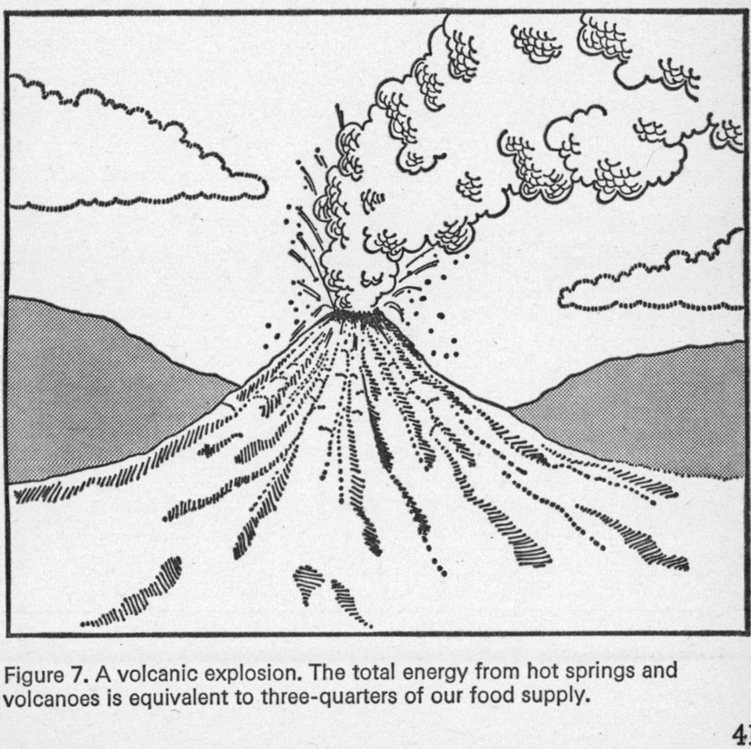

Figure 7. A volcanic explosion. The total energy from hot springs and volcanoes is equivalent to three-quarters of our food supply.

be surprising to learn that the hot-springs and volcanoes, producing together 3×10^8 kW ($2{\cdot}3 \times 10^{15}$ kcal) per year, deliver the calorific equivalent of three-quarters of all the food we are living on (see Figure 7).

Last, but by no means least, there is the kinetic energy of the Earth's rotation, an overwhelming potential of energy but one that seems impossible to exploit. The large mass of our globe means that this energy is about 10^{26} kW, nearly 10^{12} times the useful solar energy falling on our planet during the same time. We shall refrain from expressing this fantastic power in terms of man's present food and power requirements or any other such trivial quantities.

If the Moon (with its mass of $7{\cdot}3 \times 10^{22}$ kilograms) were placed on the surface of the Earth, it could be lifted up 40 times per second to the top of our highest summit, Mount Everest (8848 metres high), by the power of the Earth's rotation, and this would have a braking effect. But there is little chance of the globe coming to a standstill for, even if we could abstract from the power of its rotation *all* the energy used by mankind in his history, it would lose only one part in 10^{10} of its annual rotational energy. This proportion would be, in relation to the total weight of mankind, as if one boy were thrown into space.

A big bang

The loudest noise ever recorded on the Earth was the sound of the explosive eruption of the volcano Krakatoa in the Eastern Archipelago, in 1883, which was heard by a coastguard on Rodriguez Island about 5000 kilometres (a good 3000 miles) away across the Indian Ocean. He heard a distant booming some four hours after the explosion occurred; it is estimated that the noise must have been heard over seven per cent of the Earth's surface – the area of the USA and Canada combined.

Erosion

In the course of the last 200 years something like one-third of the USA's average 25 centimetres (10 inches) of topsoil has been lost through erosion. By 1940 it was already being estimated that, in its relatively short career as a nation, the USA had 'destroyed' an agricultural area, equal to that of Texas and New Mexico together (not far short of the combined areas of France and Spain) – at least one million square kilometres, about 250 million acres. According to a report to Congress, the process continues with a daily loss of soil equivalent to 200 farms, each of 16 hectares (40 acres).

In another part of the world, the 'Yellow' Sea gets its colour from earth eroded from the neighbouring land of China.

A threat from space

In 1908 something fell from the sky and landed in a remote part of Siberia, devastating the forest 25 kilometres (15 miles) around – altogether an area the size of Nottingham, or half as big as Long Island, New York. But no single crater has ever been found, so the nature of this object is still something of a mystery. Near Winslow, Arizona (USA) the fall of a very large meteorite left a clear trace: a nearly circular pit 1·2 kilometres across and 175 metres (575 feet) deep, with material heaped round the edge to a height of 40 metres (130 feet). At the bottom are the remains of the meteorite. Perhaps the object which landed in Siberia was also a meteorite, or perhaps it was something much more unusual – an ice-comet or possibly 'anti-matter' with reversed electrical properties (positive electrons and negative protons).

Whatever it was, the object that fell to the Earth in Siberia must have weighed something like 12,000 tonnes, as much as a loaded ocean-going cargo liner, striking the Earth at the (very) supersonic speed of 40 kilometres per second – about 150,000 kilometres per hour (90,000 m.p.h.). This would generate energy on impact amounting to $2{\cdot}7 \times 10^9$ kilowatt hours, which approaches the total power consumption (coal, oil and gas) of the UK in a year, but all released in a fraction of a second.

In nuclear energy terms, the impact of the Siberian meteorite was equivalent to 100,000 'Hiroshima' bombs, each of those being equal to 20,000 tonnes of TNT, or $2{\cdot}4 \times 10^7$ kW h. It is interesting to note that, whereas the cargo liner is extremely bulky (its overall length is more than 100 metres, or 300 feet), each of these bombs had the size of a small apple of five centimetres diameter. 100,000 such apples piled up loosely would occupy a volume of ten cubic metres, the size of a washroom in one of these ships.

The world's greatest buildings

Let us look at some notable buildings, the greatest examples of man's labour and skill (see Figure 8):

The Great Pyramid of Cheops in Egypt, which was built in about 2600 B.C., with its height of 146 metres (481 feet) contains enough stone to construct a wall around the Earth, with a thickness of one brick (20 centimetres, or 8 inches) and half a metre (20 inches) high.

In the course of the following two millennia, the Chinese must have acquired not only a formidable engineering technique, but also a prodigious supply of labour – presumably slaves – to construct the famous *Great Wall of China*. The material used in this massive construction – as long as the distance from Oslo to Naples, or from New York to New Orleans – would be enough to run our brick wall round the Earth twenty times as high as the 'Pyramid' wall.

Later on, around A.D. 1000, Indians living near the site of the present Mexico City built their magnificent *Pyramid of the Sun*; but if the material contained in this were used to build a wall around the Earth, it would be like a narrow causeway, only 15 centimetres (or 6 inches) above the ground.

Although modesty is not, perhaps, one of the most noticeable features of modern man it is remarkable that all the concrete and steel in the largest building of our time, the *Pentagon* in Washing-

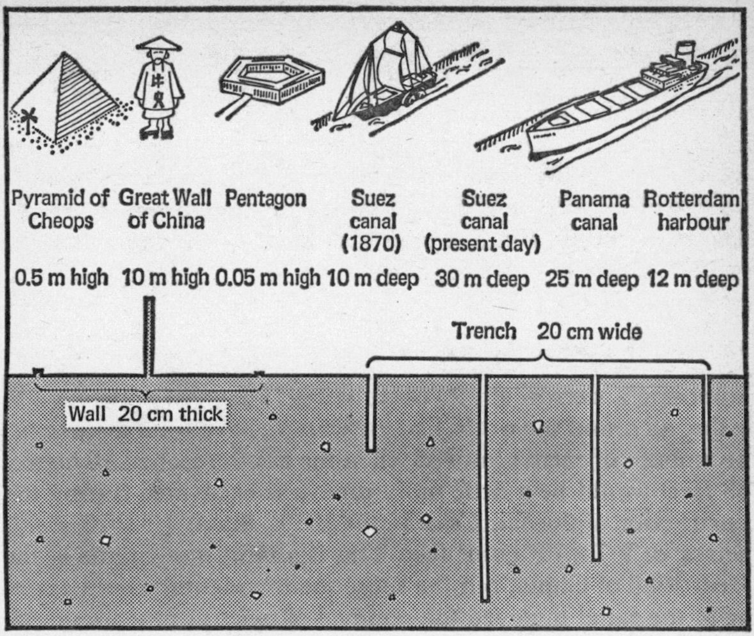

Figure 8. The quantity of material used for some of the world's greatest buildings can be expressed in terms of the height of a wall 20 centimetres thick, running all the way round the Earth. Similarly, the volume of earth excavated from canals can be measured as the depth of a 20 centimetres trench.

ton, DC, which houses the US Government's War Department, would make a 'one-brick' wall only five centimetres (two inches) high. This is because our modern buildings are hollow, not solid structures like the ancient ones. This contrast also reflects the ways in which warfare has changed over the centuries. The Wall, massive and solid, was occupied by a multitude of armed men; the Pentagon, hollow (or, better, cellular) with offices – or 'cells' – is occupied by a multitude of brains.

What sort of edifice would be large enough to contain the total volume of *all the buildings* – houses, offices, farms, factories and everything else – which now stand on the Earth? The consensus of expert opinion is that the volume available to the average man is something between 50 and 100 cubic metres per individual which includes *all* hollow spaces, rooms and corridors alike. Even the highest of these two figures means that only 350 cubic kilometres of constructed accommodation exist on the Earth. A single edifice of this volume, providing housing for the whole world would, if it was one kilometre high, cover an area roughly the size of the Isle of Wight, or twice the area of the District of Columbia in the USA, 350 square kilometres (135 square miles).

Digging the world's canals

Supposing a narrow slit 20 centimetres (8 inches) wide were to be dug all round the world like the wall we have been discussing; the amount of earth removed when the depth reached 10 metres (33 feet) would be a little more than was excavated during the construction of the *Suez Canal* in the 1870s, that is $7{\cdot}5 \times 10^7$ cubic metres, or $2{\cdot}7 \times 10^9$ cubic feet. This is almost the volume of the Great Wall of China, but the subsequent widening and deepening of the canal involved the removal of twice as much material as was dug out in the first place, making our slit round the world 30 metres (100 feet) deep (see Fig. 8).

The *Panama Canal*, reaching from sea to sea, is only about half this length but even when it was first dug it displaced nearly as much material as the enlarged Suez Canal; at an estimated $18{\cdot}5 \times 10^7$ cubic metres, the corresponding slit would be 25 metres deep.

In Europe, the recent extensions of Europoort, near Rotterdam in the Netherlands, meant the excavation of even more material than was moved to make the first Suez Canal, and the slit would be 12 metres (40 feet) deep for the docks and basins alone.

One man's field

Despite the fact that nearly three-quarters of the Earth's surface is covered by water, there would still be four hectares (ten acres) of land for every inhabitant of the world if it were shared equally between them all: five football pitches, if you could claim them! But of your four-hectare field, three would probably be too cold, too mountainous, too barren or too dry for cultivation.

So only a single hectare ($2\frac{1}{2}$ acres) per person is really available for food production. At the moment we are using only one-half of this and, moreover, of this half-hectare more than one-tenth needs artificial irrigation. In real terms, this is a total productive area the size of the State of Minnesota, about nine times that of Great Britain (200 million hectares, or 770,000 square miles altogether).

City life

Let us take Paris as an example of a big capital city:

The population, about ten million, equals the total of the 33 next largest cities in France.

Twenty per cent of France's population is crowded into the 1200 square kilometres of Paris, which cover only 0·2 per cent of the country's land surface.

In the traffic-bound centre of the city, a car is no quicker than a push-bike.

Every morning a million people – equivalent to the population of another large city – travel to join the three million local workers in the centre, then travel home again in the evening.

Within a few decades a man living on the northern outskirts of Paris might well be able to reach an office in Brussels by high-speed train more quickly than a neighbour going to *his* office on the south side of Paris. And a friend living near to a Paris airport will find it easier to cross the Channel by plane to work near a London airport than to cross Paris by car to reach his office.

Is suburban life an advantage? Fifteen per cent of one's working life is spent travelling to and from work. On the other hand, the city dwellers can enjoy squares and parks, which together with the street, represent 25 per cent of the area of Paris or London, and 35 per cent of New York.

Is there enough to drink?

Of all the $1{\cdot}3 \times 10^9$ cubic kilometres of water on the Earth, 97 per cent is in the seas and oceans, and two per cent is frozen in the polar ice-caps (and in glaciers), leaving only one per cent for us to use. But only about four per cent of this is really at our disposal – the 500,000 km^3 in rivers and (freshwater) lakes.

Even this would fill the Red Sea twice over, and it would serve our present needs for 1000 years, if only we could collect it all. Since we cannot do this we should be more careful with such a precious commodity than to use it in our WCs; the average nine litres (two gallons) used in each 'flush' represents a considerable proportion of our daily water requirements. Fortunately, only a small proportion of the world's population makes regular use of a WC. If we all had modern plumbing, five visits a day and a little hand-washing would mean that ten per cent of our 500 cubic kilometre allowance would disappear down the drain – probably to be used as domestic water somewhere else, or even as drinking water (see page 126).

Baths – as opposed to showers or douches – are another extravagance. A nice hot bath may well account for 400 litres (100 gallons), and if everyone had a daily bath our entire water supply would be used up very quickly.

Ice and snow

There are something like 30 million cubic kilometres of ice on the Earth (ten per cent of the contents of the Atlantic Ocean) and 90 per cent of it is in the Antarctic ice-cap.

In spite of its low density, snow occupies only 10,000 cubic kilometres on a world-wide year-round average, but during winter in the northern hemisphere it can cover one-quarter of the Earth's entire surface and can persist for more than four months over an area of 35 million square kilometres, nearly four times the area of the USA. If all the ice above sea-level were to melt the sea would rise by 40 metres (130 feet) so that flat coastal regions and a good many islands would disappear. Harbours would vanish under the water, leaving only the church-towers for mooring boats. A place like Worcester, well up the river Severn, would become a deep-water port.

Although the movement of glaciers and ice-sheets is very slow, in the 1930s an ice-sheet in Spitzbergen moved 20 kilometres (12 miles) in three years over a front 30 kilometres (18 miles) wide; in more familiar terms, a sheet rather larger than the Isle of Wight advanced a distance of 18 metres (60 feet) per day.

Evaporators: a lake, a wood, and a man

In a temperate climate with moderate winds, water evaporates from the surface of a lake or a sea at a rate of 15,000 litres per hectare (1300 gallons per acre) each day. This quantity would fill a small 15-seater bus. But from the leaves and twigs of a nearby beech wood, 200,000 litres per hectare (17,500 gallons per acre) would evaporate, in the same day, enough to fill thirteen or fourteen buses: one very important effect of a wood or forest on the local climate.

We can also express evaporation in terms of the rate at which the water level would be lowered:

For a lake or sea in a temperate climate the level would drop half a metre per year.

For a lake or sea in a tropical climate it would drop two metres per year.

For a beech wood in a temperate climate the drop would be seven metres per year.

A man's capacity for evaporation is only one litre of water per day, from respiration and perspiration. So from an average hectare of New York City with 90 residents, the total rate is only 0·6 per cent of the loss from the lake and 0·04 per cent of the loss from the beech wood, both in a temperate climate. However, in an underground or subway train, packed with three people per square metre, the evaporation rate increases to twice that of the lake, but is still only 14 per cent of that from the beech wood.

If water had a smell

If water molecules smelt as bad as ethanethiol does (C_2H_5SH – a constitution resembling that of alcohol, C_2H_5OH), we would live in an unbearable atmosphere. Sanitary inspectors might try to dry it with one of the most effective desiccatives known, phosphorus (V) oxide (P_2O_5). But even if the vapour pressure around us, which at 0 °C is still five millimetres of mercury, were reduced half a million times (to 10^{-5} mm of mercury), the atmosphere would still contain 3×10^{11} water molecules per cubic centimetre. Unfortunately we can still smell ethanethiol in a concentration 100 times lower. If we took a sniff of air containing ethanethiol at this low concentration, there are still 2×10^{13} of these stinkers striking each square centimetre of our sense organ per second, 5000 times as many as there are people living on Earth. So the sanitary inspectors would have to look for something more powerful than P_2O_5, but in the meantime practically all living matter would have been completely dried out.

The weight of the atmosphere

The cook has done her work well and the soufflé is 'as light as air'. But how light is air? Though we seldom really notice it, the weight of the air above us generates a pressure of one kilogram per square centimetre (about 14½ lb per square inch) at sea-level, which is exerted in all directions and indeed transmitted to the interior of all living bodies, including our own.* But let us imagine that the air exactly above us has the properties of a solid, and that the air around can exert no 'sideways' pressure; now we are staggering under a weight on our head and shoulders equal to that of a medium-sized car, 1000 kilograms (one tonne). Now let us imagine air in its liquid form; the resulting world-wide layer would be about ten metres (33 feet) deep, so that most

*Total weight of the atmosphere 5×10^{18} kilograms.

houses would be submerged. The relative contributions of the main components of this flood would be:

Nitrogen constitutes 78 per cent of the air, so it would be represented by a layer eight metres (26 feet) thick, reaching the gutters of the house.

Oxygen, at 21 per cent would contribute another two metres (6½ feet), from the gutters nearly to the chimney top.

Argon (and other inert gases), at nearly 1 per cent add the thickness of the skirting-boards, about 10 centimetres (4 inches).

Water and carbon dioxide, so important in living matter, would form almost negligible layers. Water would swamp a carpet 2½ centimetres (1 inch) thick, and the carbon dioxide layer, half a centimetre thick (less than ¼ inch), would be as thin as the linoleum on the floor.

4 The overwhelming universe

An orientation in space

Large . . .

The observable universe is the part of space that we can 'see' with our instruments and hence the part that we know something about for certain. It is an *immense* volume, with a diameter of about 10^{23} kilometres, nearly 8×10^{18} times that of the Earth. Such a volume is hard to visualise, but some impression of what 8×10^{18} times means can be gained when we think of Lake Ontario, one of the world's major lakes, which contains 1600 cubic kilometres (395 cubic miles) of water*, i.e. only $1{\cdot}6 \times 10^{18}$ cubic centimetres.

To put it another way, the diameter of the observable universe (nearly 10^{23} km) spans about 2·5 times as many light years (each equal to $9{\cdot}5 \times 10^{12}$ km) as there are people living on the Earth (4×10^{9}).

. . . and empty

Opinions differ about how *empty* the universe really is. Let us start with the assumption that there is one elementary particle† per 4 litres in the universe as a whole, including all the heavenly bodies (which make up less than one per cent of the total mass).

Therefore the number of molecules in one cubic centimetre of water (3×10^{22}) is to the number of particles in 1 cm^3 of the observable universe ($2{\cdot}2 \times 10^{-4}$) as the volume, not just of all the water in Lake Ontario but of 100 times all the water on earth, is to 1 cm^3 of water.

*This volume is 4500 times that of Lake Windermere.

† Protons, neutrons and electrons. Their total number is estimated at 10^{80} and the volume of the observable universe at $4{\cdot}5 \times 10^{83}$ cubic centimetres, so there is approximately one particle per 4·5 litres on the average.

The vast majority of the 10^{80} particles assumed to constitute the observable universe are in the fourth state of aggregation as plasma in the interior of stars. Only an infinitesimal fraction, perhaps one per cent, is organised in the form of atoms and molecules (mainly in the planets): there is still chaos!

Most of matter is found in large clusters – the galaxies – moving away from us and from each other at speeds proportional to their distances; the usual explanation is that the universe is expanding.

Stars that pass in the night[9]

Imagine fifteen grains of wheat evenly distributed over the area of Great Britain and Ireland: they would be about 200 kilometres (120 miles) apart. If a grain represented a star, it would have to be moving at no more than a small fraction of a millimetre every year to represent the movements of a group of stars within a galaxy. The chances of an interstellar collision or a 'near-miss' are no greater than the chances of our grains of wheat bumping into each other.

The Earth, just peanuts

Most of us believe that we live on an *enormous* globe, but on the scale of the universe, the Earth is a negligible object: the mass of the universe (3×10^{55} grams) contains as many times the mass of the Earth (6×10^{27} grams), as the Earth contains grams of matter. Or, to put it another way, throw two peanuts (which together weigh one gram) on to the Earth; it is as if a giant were to throw one Earth into the universe.

Creation

There are several different theories[6] concerning the origin of the universe:

No beginning and no end. The 'steady state' theory proposed by

F. Hoyle and others[7] states that the universe has always existed and has always been expanding. As galaxies move outward new ones are constantly being formed, keeping the expanding universe at a constant density. The universe is so large that, even if this 'refuelling' process created only one atom per year in a volume like that of a skyscraper, 10^{32} tonnes of matter would be created per second, more than 10^{10} times the mass equivalent of the Earth per – yes, per second!

A beginning and no end. Others believe that the universe began 10^{10} years ago in a huge explosion – a 'Big Bang' – of densely-packed matter, the fragments of which, the galaxies, now constitute the expanding universe. They are still moving outwards and, if space is infinitely large, there need be no end to this process. Just after the Big Bang, when the universe was one second old, its temperature must have been something like 15×10^9 kelvins; compared with this, the interior of the Sun (15×10^6 K) is icy cold. After a year the temperature in the region of the explosion was still at 1,000,000 kelvins and a million years later it was 3000 kelvins. Now, after some 10^{10} years, the inter-stellar space is at 50 kelvins (−223 °C), a temperature we find on Earth only in laboratories. Poetic scientists have described this temperature as 'the remnant whispers of the Big Bang of Creation'.

A beginning and an end. Other believers in the 'Big Bang' theory take the view that gravitational attraction between the galaxies will eventually overcome their outward motion, pulling the fragments back and eventually leading to a catastrophic collision, which will destroy the universe – a beginning and an end.

The most critical point in the 'Big-Bang' theory concerns the constitution of the densely-packed matter in the body which originally exploded. It was presumably composed of atomic nuclei and must have had a density of more than 10^{14} grams per cubic centimetre (see page 21), which means that a pinhead (one cubic millimetre) of this matter would weigh as much as 100,000 medium-sized automobiles. This extreme density of 10^{14} is very much greater than the mean density of matter in the universe as a whole, which is about 10^{-27} gram per cubic centimetre. It means that our pinhead of nuclear material would weigh as much as 10^{44} pinheads of space, a volume equivalent to that of a cube with sides three times the distance separating us from the Sun (length of side = $4{\cdot}5 \times 10^8$ kilometres).

Repeating beginnings and ends. Yet another concept is that of the 'oscillating' universe which – having expanded after the Big Bang – will contract to an extremely dense state and then move outward again in a never-ending cycle of 8×10^{10} years. This cycle has been fancifully called 'the breathing of Atman' (the world spirit). If this theory is true we shall have to wait 7×10^{10} years – seven times the present age of the universe – before the galaxies will come together again to begin the next cycle, with never an end in sight. Within the pattern of this cycle our own stellar system is estimated to have been in existence something like 5×10^9 years. This is a period similar to that which, in certain other theories has elapsed since the Earth began to condense from a gas cloud, $4{\cdot}7 \times 10^9$ years being the estimate for the time since the Earth began to solidify.

A critical scientist might wonder whether theories of never-ending cycles would not be in conflict with the basic conception of thermodynamics concerning the impossibility of a *perpetuum mobile.* This is currently a subject of serious study.[8]

	Diameter	*Mass*
Earth	$1{\cdot}27 \times 10^4$ km	6×10^{24} kg
Sun	$1{\cdot}4 \times 10^6$ km	2×10^{30} kg
Milky Way (longest axis)	$7{\cdot}5 \times 10^{17}$ km	2×10^{41} kg
Observable universe	$4{\cdot}3 \times 10^{22}$ km	3×10^{52} kg

1 light year = $9{\cdot}5 \times 10^{12}$ km.

Within our solar system

The present is the past

The cosmologist – more than any other scientist – is aware that when he looks into the night sky he is looking into the past. This is because even the nearest stars are immense distances from

Earth, and although light travels very quickly it still takes an appreciable time to reach us. So we see the Moon as it was 1¼ seconds earlier. For the Sun this period is 8½ minutes; for the nearest star it is four years; and light now reaching us from the nearest galaxy set off at a time when our distant forefathers were first appearing on Earth, some 2½ million years ago.

Some mass-relationships

Suppose that the mass of the human body (70 kilograms, or 150 lb) represents the mass of our whole solar system. The Sun is the giant of the system, containing 99·8 per cent of the total mass, leaving only 0·2 per cent or 140 grams (the mass of one little finger) for all the other bodies revolving around it, i.e. the planets, their satellites and the asteroids. In this picture the Earth is represented by the mass of the nail on that little finger, 0·3 gram. What can we learn from this comparison, with the human body standing for the whole solar system? Simply this: the mass of the solar system is roughly related to that of a man as the mass of a man is related to that of a hydrogen molecule. But since, as we said, the mass of the Sun is practically equal to that of our whole solar system, we can replace the term 'solar system' in this equation simply by 'Sun'.

Mass of our solar system = 2×10^{30} kg.
Mass of a hydrogen molecule = $3{\cdot}4 \times 10^{-27}$ kg.

Breathless space

People who climb mountains know very well that as they go higher the air becomes rarer. At the top of Mount Everest (8848 metres or 29,028 feet above sea-level) the density of the air is only about one-third of that at sea-level. Other things being equal, a man must breathe three times as fast – 45 deep breaths per minute – to get the same amount of oxygen into his system. What would an astronaut's lungs have to do if his supply of air or oxygen should fail? Let us follow him on a journey to the Moon.

On Earth his breathing rate is 15 breaths per minute.

Ten kilometres (33,000 feet) up the rate would be 45 breaths per minute.

A hundred kilometres (62 miles up), he would have to breathe one million times as fast as he does on the surface. To inhale one minute's supply of air he would have to breathe for two years at the normal rate or else he could speed up his rate of breathing to the frequency of radio-waves, 3×10^5 times per second.

A thousand kilometres (620 miles) up, with only one four-hundredth of the Moon trip completed he would have to start breathing at the time the Earth began to solidify, 4700 million years ago, to obtain his usual one-minute quota at the normal rate of 15 breaths per minute. Alternatively he could adopt high-speed breathing at the frequency of the radiation we know as visible light, 10^{15} times per second.

Once he reaches the Moon life becomes easier, although for his first minute after landing it would have helped if he had begun breathing two months before his arrival in order to inhale his earthly one-minute quota. Again, the problem could be solved by faster breathing, at the relatively leisurely frequency of the longer radio-waves, about $2{\cdot}5 \times 10^4$ times per second.

Density of the atmosphere (approximate number of molecules per cubic centimetre)	
On the Earth's surface	3×10^{19}
10 kilometres (33,000 feet) up	1×10^{19}
100 kilometres (62 miles) up	3×10^{13}
1000 kilometres (620 miles) up	1×10^4
On the Moon	3×10^{14}

The Sun is shining

The Sun is a gaseous nuclear-power plant, emitting some 4×10^{23} kilowatts or 10^{23} kilocalories per second by converting hydrogen into helium, nuclear particles and energy. To appreciate this prodigious flood of power let us suppose that all this emitted energy could be collected on the Earth; a single square centimetre of the Earth's surface would then receive more than enough to satisfy the present food and power consumption of a city the size of Durham, with 30,000 inhabitants.

Fortunately, because of its great distance from the Sun and its surrounding atmosphere the Earth's surface intercepts only a tiny fraction of this power: 3×10^{13} kcal per second ($1{\cdot}21 \times 10^{14}$ kW see page 37). If it was not thus protected no life would be possible on Earth.

Although the rate of hydrogen transformation per second amounts to something like the load capacity of 6000 supertankers each of 100,000 tons ($6{\cdot}1 \times 10^{8}$ tonnes), it seems that the Sun's power might last for another 10,000 million years. However, it is believed that only a fraction of this hydrogen on the Sun will actually be consumed before a new process based on transmutation into heavier elements (e.g. carbon) begins. We can expect this within 5000 million years.

Harnessing the Sun's power

Up until now very little use has been made of the stream of energy reaching our globe from the Sun (see page 68), but modern research, especially in space*, has led to a promising new development.

Plans now exist to collect solar radiation by means of lightweight satellites placed in a synchronous orbit round the Earth, and to convert the energy captured in these solar collectors into direct current power. This will be concentrated into microwaves and beamed by an antenna to a receiving antenna of a similar size on Earth, which will convert the microwave power back into d.c. power. The wavelength of the microwaves is between 10 and 20 centimetres which allows a penetration through our

*Two other promising projects are: to convert the solar energy in deserts into electricity by means of photo-electric cells[12, 13], or to operate a buoyant heat engine between the warm upper layer and the colder deep water of the tropical oceans.[14]

Figure 9. Special panels on the roof of this house trap solar energy, which can then be used for heating purposes.

atmosphere with a very low loss, even under the worst cloud and precipitation conditions. Recent estimates[10] are that for every square metre of collector-panel the Earth will receive 0·15 kilowatts. The present electricity requirements of some consumption areas could be met by satellites of the following approximate sizes:

For the USA, consuming 10^8 kW, a panel of 650 square kilometres (250 square miles) would be needed; that is four times the area of the District of Columbia.

For Western Europe consuming 6×10^7 kW the panel would have to be 400 km^2 (150 square miles) – the size of the Isle of Wight.

The electrical consumption of the whole world ($2{\cdot}8 \times 10^8$ kW) would require a panel of 1800 km^2 (700 square miles) – half the size of great Salt Lake in the USA or 1·3 times the Isle of Rhodes in the Mediterranean Sea.

The project is still in its infancy and it is hard to predict the impact which it will have on man's future energy supply. One of the biggest problems is how to transport such large collectors and transmitters into orbit over a distance of 35,000 kilometres (nearly the circumference of the Earth) and to assemble them there, but research suggests that there may be ways of doing this[11]. An especially attractive feature of this method of obtaining energy is that pollution from burning fuels is avoided.

Sunspots

During a typical eruption on the surface of the Sun, amounts of energy up to 10^{22} kilocalories (4×10^{25} joules) are observed to be stored in distortions of the magnetic field. This is enough to bring one-third of the water in the Atlantic Ocean to the boil.

Holding our neighbours fast

The force of the gravitational attraction between the Earth and

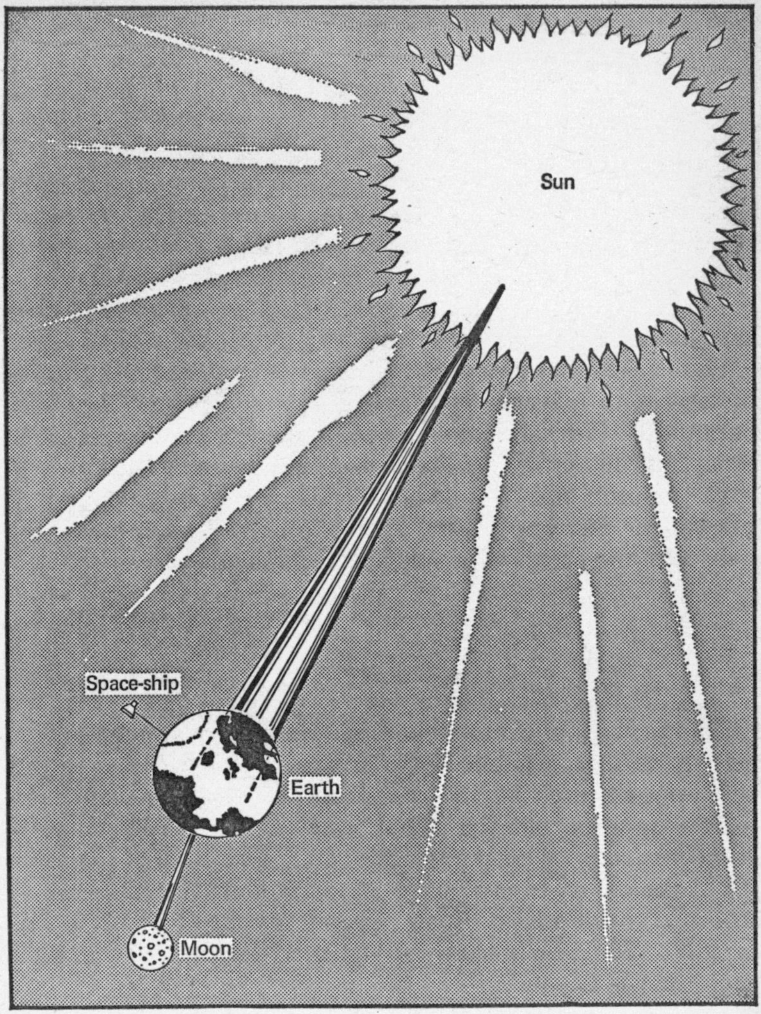

Figure 10. Gravity expressed as a steel bar: to hold the Moon the bar would need to have a cross-section the size of California; for the Sun it would have to be nearly as big as the Atlantic Ocean; to hold a spaceship a bar the width of your little finger-nail would be enough.

the Moon is the same as the strength of a gigantic steel bar* of cross-section 400,000 square kilometres, the area of California. But the corresponding force between the Sun and the Earth is as strong as a steel bar of cross-section about 75,000,000 square kilometres – the area of the Indian Ocean and only slightly less than the area of the Atlantic Ocean.

On a similar scale, the gravitational force between the Earth and some future space-ship of mass ten tonnes circling the Earth 3640 kilometres away from its surface (that is, in an orbit of radius 10,000 kilometres) would be as strong as a steel bar of cross-section 0·8 square centimetre, about the area of one's little finger-nail.

It is believed that the cohesive forces within the atomic nucleus correspond to a tensile strength of 10^{21} kilograms per square centimetre. Material of this strength in the form of a rod of cross-section just under four square centimetres (roughly the area of a human thumb nail) – would sustain the gravitational pull between the Sun and Earth, a force $3{\cdot}9 \times 10^{21}$ kilograms – the strength of the ocean-wide steel bar described above.

The Earth and the Moon

Astronomers tell us that two bodies which are relatively close to each other in space like the Earth and the Moon, interact gravitationally in such a way that their rotation about each other, and the rotation of each about its own axis, will eventually become equal, so that finally each will always present the same face to the other. In our Earth–Moon system, this has already happened to the Moon. But it was not always so and it is estimated that 600 million years ago a year on Earth was two months longer than it is now.

If we did not have satellites sending back pictures, another way of getting a good look at the other side of the Moon would be to fire a really large object to strike the Moon at its apparent 'edge' – in other words, tangentially. A pyramid the height of Mount

*Steel of tensile strength 5000 kg per cm^2.

Everest (nine kilometres, or 5½ miles), seven kilometres (4½ miles) along the base, would do; if it were projected with an escape velocity of 12 kilometres (7½ miles) per second, on striking the Moon it would set it spinning, turning once every 210 days.

Saving Apollo 12 from 'burn-up'

If we want to recover vehicles from space, one of the most difficult problems is how to dissipate the heat developed during the 'slowing down' stage, after the vehicle has entered the upper layers of the Earth's atmosphere. The speed of entry is usually in the region of 40,000 kilometres per hour (24,000 m.p.h.) On the Earth's surface this would take a traveller right round the Equator in one hour. 'Slowing down' from this speed means that kinetic energy is being transformed into heat on the scale of 15,000 kilocalories per kilogram mass of the vehicle.

The Apollo 12 vehicle that explored the Moon in 1970 had a mass of 5000 kilograms, so that the total heat to be dissipated on its entry into the Earth's atmosphere was 15,000 × 5000 which is 75 million kcal: enough heat to melt 300 tonnes of iron, the quantity in a fair-sized coaster. This explains why early proposals to cool a returning space-vehicle with water proved to be quite impractical; vehicle, crew and water would all be turned to vapour.

The answer is to make the re-entry vehicle a shape which will cause most of the heat to be absorbed by the surrounding air, leaving only a small proportion to be taken up by the vehicle itself. This shape is the now familiar truncated cone. At blast-off the narrow end leads, but before re-entering the Earth's atmosphere the vehicle turns so that the wide end is leading. This end carries the heat-shield, a layer of plastic several centimetres thick, and after the turn the shape of the vehicle is *anti*-streamlined to give maximum air-resistance during the descent.

When molecules of air are struck by the heat-shield – moving, as we saw, at about 40,000 kilometres per hour – they rebound with an even greater velocity into the nearby air, imparting their energy to other molecules; so about a metre in front of the heat-shield a zone of very hot compressed air is formed – a 'shock wave' – in which a temperature of 6000 °C, is reached, the temperature of the surface of the Sun itself. The heat that develops in this shock-wave and its subsequent dissipation in the surrounding atmosphere absorbs an estimated 99 per cent of all the heat evolved; of the remaining one per cent, nine-tenths evaporates the material of the heat-shield, and only one-tenth has to be absorbed by the main structure of the vehicle. The outside can still reach a temperature of 300 °C, however.

The tremendous amount of heat that has to be dissipated during the re-entry period of the space-ship may be seen from this example. The human body is generally at a higher temperature than its surroundings and so people themselves radiate heat. An active man might give out some 100 kilocalories per hour. Now the re-entry of the Apollo capsule through the Earth's atmosphere takes 15 minutes, during which time a man could radiate 25 kcal. The dissipation of 75 million kcal by the space vehicle, carrying three people, is therefore equivalent to the heat radiated by some three million active persons: about the number of inhabitants of Eire or Uruguay.

The Moon travel bill

The first Moon-landing (1969), including the comprehensive preparations during a five-year period, cost a total of about 20,000 million dollars, i.e. an average expenditure of $20 a year for each American. A chemist has calculated that this is approximately the same rate of spending in the USA as on hair lotions, lipsticks, and other beauty preparations.

5 Plants and animals[15]

Biological specimens made visible

Let us imagine a flea on a man's head or – more hygienically – on a football (diameter 22 centimetres, or 8·5 inches). If the football is now increased to the size of the Earth (diameter 12,700 kilmetres or 7900 miles) and the flea is enlarged in the same proportion (58 million times), what would an observer be able to see?

The flea (1·5 millimetres or 1/20 inch long) would cover an area equal to that of Delaware, one of the smallest states in the USA, or that of the county of Lincolnshire: 6000 square kilometres, or 2400 square miles.

A single mammalian *cell* (diameter 0·1 millimetre) would be seen as a smaller city like Norwich, or Albany (NY) in the USA (27 square kilometres, or about 10 square miles).

The *nucleus* in this cell (diameter 0·01 millimetre) would cover a fair-sized park such as Green Park in London, or the park around City Hall, New York (250,000 square metres, or 300,000 square yards).

In this same cell a *mitochondrion* (diameter 0·001 millimetre), where food is converted into energy, would have the appearance of a substantial building, with an area of 2500 square metres (3100 square yards); it would be a little larger than the White House, the official home of the President of the USA.

Also within the cell, one would be able to distinguish *spiral molecules of DNA* (deoxyribonucleic acid) which are really about 0·017 millimetre long and 2×10^{-6} millimetres wide. They would appear as very long but narrow footpaths in the park, 15 centimetres (6 inches) wide, and 1 kilometre (0·6 mile) long.

Outside (or possibly within) the cell there might be a specimen of *Bacillus coli* ($1{\cdot}5 \times 10^{-3}$ millimetre in diameter). This would be seen on our magnified scale as a gigantic flying saucer covering 6000 square metres (7200 square yards), between the size of a hockey pitch and a football pitch.

A *smallpox virus* (diameter $1{\cdot}5 \times 10^{-4}$ millimetre), taking up the area of a small house, 65 square metres or 77 square yards, is still large compared with the *yellow fever virus* (diameter 2×10^{-5} millimetre) which could be fitted into the smallest room in the house, one metre ($3\frac{1}{3}$ feet) square.

Haemoglobin, with a molecule $5{\cdot}5 \times 10^{-6}$ millimetre is even smaller and would be seen as a large floor-tile, 30 centimetres square (1 square foot) in the 'smallest room'.

On seeing a *saccharose molecule*, 7×10^{-7} millimetre, our observer would think that there was a mouse 3·6 centimetres across (1·5 inches) sitting on the tile.

Finally, there is a *molecule of water*: its real diameter $1{\cdot}7 \times 10^{-8}$ centimetre, is magnified to the size of a large drop of water on the tile, nearly one centimetre square (0·15 square inch).

The largest living things

Plants

The largest single living object on the Earth is one of the Sequoia Pines growing in California, USA: it has been named after the great Federal soldier, General Wm. T. Sherman. At its base the circumference is 31 metres (102 feet), so that the outstretched arms of 17 men would be needed to encircle it; and the whole tree contains enough wood – 1200 cubic metres (42,400 cubic feet) – to make 35 five-roomed bungalows.

The seed of such a tree weighs only 0·01 gram (1/3000 of an ounce): its growth to a mature tree therefore represents an

Figure 11. Man and car framed by the base of one of the world's largest trees. Trees of this size grow in the Sequoia National Park, California.

increase in weight of 100,000 million fold. This is ten times the increase from the weight of a human egg-cell to the weight of a fully-grown man. Even so, the height of the 'General Sherman' Sequoia (83 metres, 272 feet, or 45 average men standing one above another) is only half the height of the tallest tree known, a Eucalyptus (155 metres, or 500 feet high) – the equivalent of 85 men standing one above another.

Animals

In terms of weight, the mightiest animal that has ever lived is the blue whale; a specimen weighing 125 tonnes and measuring 29 metres (96 feet) in length was caught in 1931. This is equal to the weight of 4 brontosauri, 23 elephants, 230 cows or 1800 men – whichever you prefer. But the whale occupied only one-tenth of the volume of the 'General Sherman' Sequoia.

Photosynthesis[16]

Photosynthesis produces carbon compounds in the leaves of plants and stores energy in the form of carbohydrates like starch, sugar and wood, which are 45 per cent carbon. With a few minor exceptions, all the world's food depends on the green plant, and the plant's growth in turn depends on photosynthesis, and *that* depends on solar radiation.

As we saw on page 37, each year the Earth is flooded with $9{\cdot}50 \times 10^{20}$ kilocalories of potentially useful energy from the Sun, which means an average of 5000 kcal per day on every square metre (1·2 square yards) of land *and* sea. If this could be converted into food, a single square metre of the Earth's surface could feed two people all the year round (Figure 12).

Unfortunately only about 0·03 per cent of this potentially useful power stream is directly involved in supporting life and, because of the inefficiency of the photo-chemical reaction, only a small fraction (0·1 per cent) of this is fixed by photosynthesis. It is astonishing that although huge numbers of plants have depended for 2000 million years upon photosynthesis as their

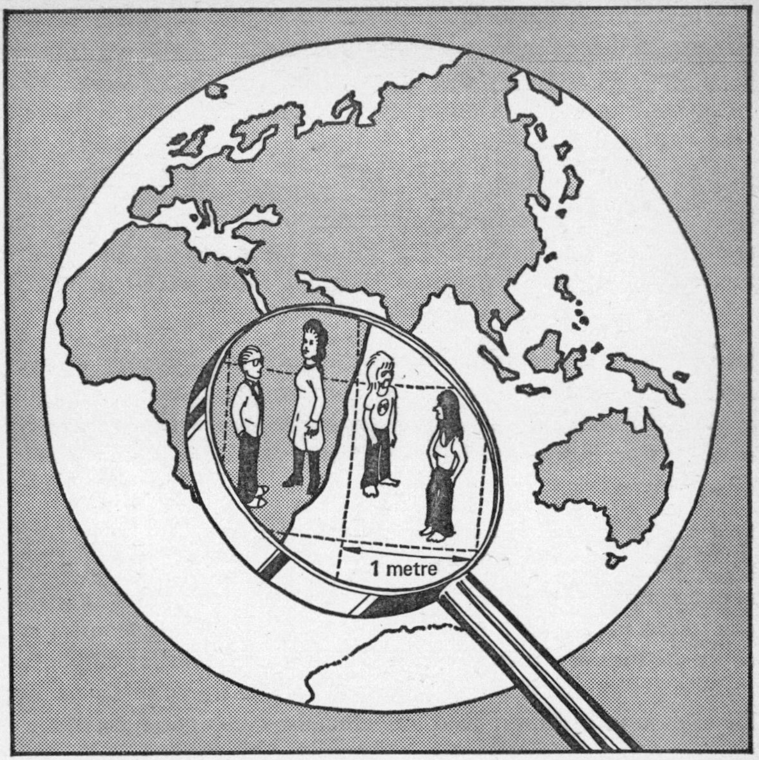

Figure 12. Theoretically, the Sun supplies enough energy to feed everyone on Earth, even if it were densely packed with two people per square metre (22 per square yard) over its entire surface – land and sea.

sole method of capturing energy, they have not succeeded in developing a higher level of efficiency than this. It is even more surprising when we learn that other biological processes are much more efficient. The human body, for instance, converts fuel (food) at our body temperature into energy with 15 per cent efficiency, which is better than the 12 per cent rate of several cylinder locomotives which operate at 300 °C (572 °F). For the solar energy which actually reaches the plants, even good farming reaches an efficiency of no more than one per cent – a challenge to agricultural research!

The situation has been summed up in this way: the 'highly efficient' fixing of energy by good farming amounts to no more than one day's supply out of the whole growing season. This disappointing performance is further emphasised in the following observations:

The 8×10^{17} kilocalories ($3{\cdot}5 \times 10^{20}$ joules) fixed annually in the form of carbohydrates on our entire globe represent an efficiency of only 0·1 per cent which is 250 times as bad as that of the first steam engine built by James Watt in 1788, which delivered 1 kcal of power by burning 38 kcal of coal.

Each year Man extracts from the incoming energy shower $3{\cdot}6 \times 10^{15}$ kcal of food to live on. This means that only one out of every 250,000 useful kilocalories sent to us is actually eaten by man. It is as if in a city like Newcastle only one single person is doing any work.

Our actual consumption of carbon in the form of coal, oil and gas is estimated at 7×10^{9} tonnes per year. So if the 10^{11} tonnes of carbon present in the carbohydrates formed per year could be converted into these fuels, 15 times our annual fuel consumption could be manufactured by photosynthesis. We are rapidly consuming our stocks of stored-up sunshine from the past (see below) for the simple reason that no efficient conversion method is known.

The agronomic harvest

Judging by its yield per unit area, photosynthesis seems to act in much the same way on a number of important crop types. For instance, the world yields during 1948–1953 were:

Wheat. 1000 kilograms per hectare (880 pounds per acre) per year.

Maize and rice. 1600 kilograms per hectare (1400 pounds per acre) per year.

In fact, the *total* production of dry matter (grains plus fibrous constituents) has to be considered: as a rough approximation the grain weight can be doubled.

In the moderate climate of the Midlands a square metre (1·2 square yards) receives in a year the energy equivalent of the food which an active man consumes in one day: 3000 kilocalories (12 million joules). This is the 'one day: one year' relationship.

In dry climates like those in many developing countries, the captured energy is, of course, much higher; but the conversion factor is much poorer, because of the lack of water. A figure of 0·02 per cent efficiency seems to be about the average, which gives an annual yield from a square metre sufficient to feed a man for a few hours.

Attempting to improve the world food situation by better farming leads to a paradox, formulated by Penman[16] in a striking way. Increasing the energy conversion efficiency of photosynthesis in the best farming countries by ten per cent (say from 1·0 to 1·1 per cent) would give an increase in the world's food that could only be achieved by *doubling* the output from equal areas in very poor countries, where the level is now 0·1 per cent conversion. It is self-evident that the simplest way to increase the total output is to make the best even better. And this is clearly happening in practice. During 1953–1965 the human race increased by 50 per cent, but those crop yields that rose by the same amount were unfortunately not in the hungry areas.

Of the 350,000 plant species that have so far been classified by botanists, only 3000 – not even one per cent of the total – have been tried as food. And ninety per cent of our food supply comes from a dozen or so types.

The animal harvest[17]

Many people hold the view that animals compete directly with man for food, and that it would therefore be wise to cut them from the food chain: plant →animal →man. As far as calories are concerned this may be right. Under favourable conditions (for both plants and animals) cereals yield twice as many calories as dairy farming, and it takes seven or eight kilograms of digestible feed protein to produce one kilogram of animal protein for us to eat. Nevertheless, the supply of food from animals is important because of the great variety of fats and essential amino acids that it contains. And last, but not least, there is the delicious steak au Chef!

Overall, animals contribute ten per cent of man's intake of calories, and an important argument for keeping them – especially certain ruminants – is that they can hydrolyse certain linkages of cellulose in grass or shrubs. Don Quixote's ass is the traditional example of an animal which can live on dry ground where good farming is impossible. Notwithstanding these arguments, it is perhaps surprising that more ground is available for cattle than for crops:

Nearly one-third of the Earth's surface is land.

One-third of the land is used for agriculture.

One-third of the agricultural area is arable land.

Two-thirds of the agricultural area consists of meadows and pastures.

It may also be surprising to learn that hunting still makes a measurable – albeit small – contribution to our food supply, and so does fishing. Here are the proportions concerned:

For each 70 kilograms of edible plants harvested on land, one gram is derived from the sea: the same ratio as the one between the weight of a man and the weight of one of his eyeballs.

For each kilogram of meat that the butcher sells, the poulterer and the fishmonger each sell 50 grams. The ratio in each case is that of our body weight to the weight of two fingers.

Two pieces of incidental information:

A good cow (weight 700 kilograms) produces 10,000 litres (2200 gallons) of milk per year with an energy content of $7{\cdot}5 \times 10^6$ kilocalories. That is enough for seven adults to live on. One adult could also live on the produce of three goats or a single sow.

Believe it or not, a farmer could drive his car all day long on the methane gas which his cows or sheep produce in that period (see page 85).

The sea's harvest[17, 18]

The quantity of ocean plants that grow each year ($1{\cdot}5 \times 10^{11}$ tonnes) is four times as much as that on land. But since the sea surface is 2·3 times that of all the land, the plant yield 'per hectare of sea' is 1·6 times that on land. Now what does this mean with regard to the edible food we extract from the sea? In 1964 the world catch of sea fish, including crustaceans, was 30 million tonnes – just over five per cent of the 500 million tonnes of edible food produced on land. In this comparison we must take account of the fact that on land man exerts all his efforts to obtain the maximum yield, whereas the multiplication and exploitation of the sea's potential has scarcely begun. Nearly all the fish caught come from waters over the continental shelves, which account for less than ten per cent of the total area of the oceans.

The microscopic plant life (*phytoplankton*) supports small fauna (*zooplankton*), which in its turn sustains the young fishes and the crustacea, so we find three main links in the chain:

500 kilograms of phytoplankton produce 100 kilograms of zooplankton.

100 kilograms of zooplankton produce 10 kilograms of herring.

10 kilograms of herring produce 1 kilogram of tuna fish.

This is an overall efficiency of 1 to 500.

If we could find an effective way of controlling this process, using all the phytoplankton available, and catching the herring before they are eaten by higher species like tuna fish, an annual production of 3000 million tonnes of herrings might be possible. This would mean, in terms of calories, ten times all the food that is now produced on the land. What a prospect! We could all eat 2·5 kilograms (5½ lb) of kippers every day! Our food problem would be solved for a long time.

Note

It has been calculated that a cubic metre of plankton can produce as much cattle food per year as a cubic metre of arable land, i.e.

175 grams of organic matter. Plankton has therefore been called 'a floating meadow, the humus of the ocean'.

	Tonnes per year		*kcal per year*
Potentially useful energy received by the Earth			9×10^{20}
Carbohydrates formed on land	$0{\cdot}4 \times 10^{11}$		
Carbohydrates formed in the sea	$1{\cdot}5 \times 10^{11}$		
Total	$1{\cdot}9 \times 10^{11}$	=	$7{\cdot}2 \times 10^{17}$
Edible food product on land			$8{\cdot}9 \times 10^{15}$
Edible food produced in the sea			$2{\cdot}9 \times 10^{13}$

The stored-up sunshine of the past

The mass of carbon in all living things* is estimated at $2{\cdot}5 \times 10^{11}$ tonnes[19]. Since the quantity stored in carbon dioxide in the atmosphere is only 50 per cent greater, life on Earth might be very different if it were not for the considerable amounts of carbon dissolved as salts in the sea. When these are added together, the total quantity of carbon is some 80 times that found in living things.

The total mass of carbohydrates formed in the last 500 million years (and which are mostly decomposed) is estimated at 6×10^{19} tonnes; that is one per cent of the mass of the Earth.

Only two per cent of the exhaled carbon dioxide is produced by men and animals; the rest is from microbes.

Growth in Bacterialand

The multiplying capacity of the simple micro-organisms is so enormous that we must be glad of Nature's own brakes on the process. Let us consider any member of the *coccus* type of bacteria, minute spherical objects one micron (μ) across (0·001 millimetre), of which a million million (10^{12}) would just occupy one cubic centimetre.

*So we exclude coal, oil, gas etc.

Each cell is potentially capable of dividing itself into two similar cells every half-hour. On this basis, it is theoretically possible that one cell might have 2^{48} descendants after 24 hours, and 2^{96} descendants after 48 hours.

These 2^{96} cells would have a dry weight of 10,000 million tonnes, so to transport them all at once we would need a fleet of 3300 million three-tonne trucks. Driven one behind the other they would form a procession which would go 600 times around the Equator.

We can also read[20] about *Bacterium coli*, which can split into two every eleven minutes: in three days it could produce a mass of offspring surpassing the population of the Earth.

All this is purely theoretical, however, because the growth of bacteria is limited by the availability of food-stuffs for these little organisms; in fact for the *coccus* to reproduce at the rate we described, 100 times the dry-weight of the final quantity of bacteria would be needed as food – that is one million million tonnes.

Population in Bacterialand

At a conference called to consider the problem of increasing population in the 'developing' countries, an expert from Bacterialand produces, with a smile, the following facts and figures: The number of bacteria in

One litre of drinking water is 100,000 – the same as the population of Northampton or, in the USA, Harrisburg Pa.

One litre of air in a busy town is comparable to the population of Glasgow (or Baltimore) – one million.

One litre of milk, two hours after milking, is about equivalent to the population of Belgium – ten million.

The same litre of milk three hours after milking would have grown to the size of the population of Spain – about 30 million.

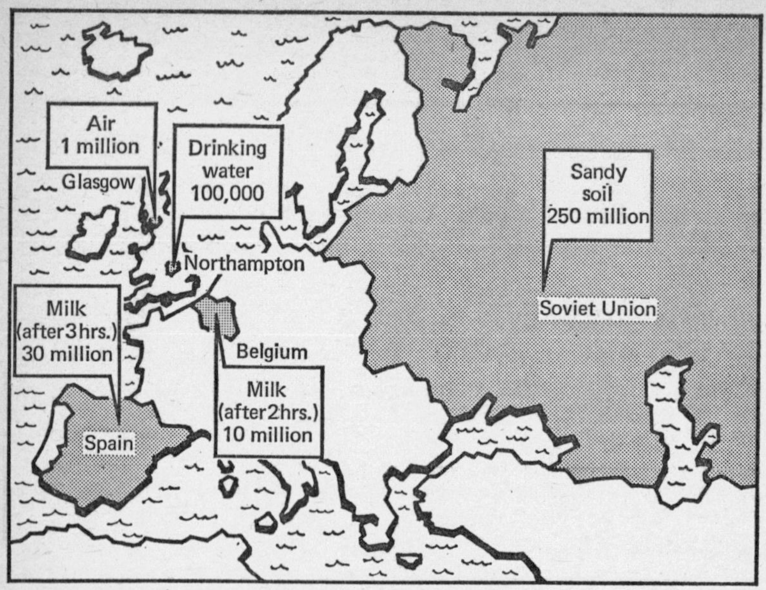

Figure 13. The number of bacteria in one litre of the substance named in the square corresponds to the population of the place indicated. In a litre of washing-up water their number is equal to one-third of all the people living (10^9), and in a litre of rich cultivated soil there is 30 times the world's population.

One litre of sandy soil is like the population of the Soviet Union, approximately 250 million.

One litre of washing-up water (after it has been used) approaches one-third of the world's population – 1000 million (10^9)*.

One litre of well-cultivated rich soil is some 30 times as large as the world's population – 100,000 million (10^{11}).

He goes on to remind the meeting of the agronomists' discovery that in every gram of fertile soil there are some 10^8 living bacteria (size about 1 μ^3). There are 200–500 kilograms of microbes to every hectare (practically the same number of pounds of microbes per acre) of good agricultural soil. The total

*1970 estimate.

mass of microbiological life has been estimated at 25 times as much as the total mass of all animal life, both aquatic and terrestrial.

He also pointed out that some areas of the human skin (e.g. the axilla) are as densely populated with micro-organisms as fertile soil with 500 million individuals per gram of scurf or soil, which gives a population density of 2·5 million *cocci* per square centimetre.

Heat from bacteria

When converting leaves and other plant waste into fertile humus, the vast micro-populations of bacteria produce heat by bio-chemical reactions. On a square metre (1·2 square yards) of rich meadow they develop over 1000 kilocalories per year, the equivalent of feeding an active person for eight hours. In an oak or a beech-wood the annual amount of heat developed per square metre equals a two- or three-hour food supply for that person. This might seem small but the heat produced in such a wood is twice the calorific equivalent of the whole annual wheat or maize harvest on a square metre in a poor country with a dry climate, like India.

Matches and a writing-desk

The wood produced in one hour by the growth of a healthy poplar-tree would be just about enough for the matches in two ordinary match-boxes, which means two matches are grown every minute. To produce a pair of Dutch clogs the tree would need a week. A good writing-desk is quite a different matter; we could use a poplar's growth for one year, but for a well-made job in oak the tree would need ten years to provide the wood.

Watering our daily bread

When we take a bath, we might run the tap for five minutes and use 400 to 500 litres of water (about 100 gallons). Stalks of grain growing in a field have to draw the same amount from the ground to produce a couple of handfuls of flour for a loaf of bread.

Minerals from the soil

Imagine a cart loaded after a good harvest. In a 25-tonne load the weight of mineral nutrients (compounds including nitrogen, phosphorus, potassium, calcium and magnesium) have a weight equal to that of five young men, 330 kilograms or 730 lb. Now, looking more carefully for those trace elements which the growing plants must extract from the ground for their proper development, viz. copper, manganese, boron, cobalt and zinc, we should find that their total weight was only 1 kg (2·2 lb).

Multiplication by animals

A queen-bee lays her eggs at the rate of one each minute; and if she could keep this up for a whole year she would lay half a million eggs.

A termite queen lays eggs at the rate of one per second, which means a total of 30 million possible offspring in a year. Observers have stated that she can keep up this colossal output for over 30 years.

The 100-mm long Giant African Snail is so prolific that if the fully-grown progeny from a three-year period of reproduction ($1{\cdot}6 \times 10^{16}$ snails) were arranged in a straight line the first- and last-born would be separated by a distance equivalent to two million trips from the Earth to the Moon (over two light months). If the young were born at the rate of one every second, the first of such a progeny would be 500 million years older than the last.

Remembering from page 75 that *Bacterium coccus* can produce 2^{48} descendants in 24 hours, the family of $1{\cdot}6 \times 10^{15}$ produced by the snail in three years would easily be produced by the *coccus* in 28 hours.

Immortality

We usually think of cold rather than warmth as a killer but raising the body temperature of many creatures, including the smallest of organisms, by 40 °C is often sufficient to extinguish any sign of life. On the other hand, *spermatozoa* and other more complicated creatures survive temperatures close to absolute zero, provided that cooling takes place very rapidly. Thus they can endure a range of nearly 313 °C. Breathing and the other bodily functions are retarded by a factor of 10^{13} when absolute zero (−273 °C) is approached, and an organism held at −272 °C achieves a state something like immortality. Under these circumstances the time factor changes dramatically: so much so that the amount of ageing that would have taken place since the Earth became solid, 3300 million years ago, would occur in the same organism kept at room temperature in one-third of a second.

Blooming after ten thousand years

The oldest seeds to have been successfully germinated and grown in the laboratory are those of an Arctic Lupin found in the Yukon Territory. At least 10,000 years old, the seeds must have been deep-frozen and covered by some insulating layer which prevented the soil from thawing. This period is twice as long as the time that has passed since the Babylonians began to write our history in 3500 B.C.

Killing insects[21]

According to the latest estimates there may be as many as three million different kinds of insects, far more than all the other animal and plant species put together. The number of individual insects alive at any one time is thought to be about a million million million (10^{18}) which means that each person could have – if he wanted to collect them – a quantity of insects equal to the population of the USA and Japan combined, 300 million. Of this vast multitude 99·9 per cent are, from our own point of view, either innocuous or downright helpful. A few are indispensable – think of the role of bees in pollination!

The troublemakers are the other 0·1 per cent (about 3000 species). They are the agricultural pests and the carriers of human and animal disease. Those that transmit human disease are the most troublesome of all; they have joined with the bacteria, viruses and protozoa in what has sometimes seemed like a grand conspiracy to exterminate man.

Various pesticides like DDT were developed to combat the insects with chemistry, but recently it was discovered that certain juvenile hormones produced by the insects themselves are extremely powerful insect destroyers. Instead of killing the insects straight away, these hormones upset the normal mechanisms of development if they come into contact with the eggs, which then fail to hatch. For example one gram of the hormone *Cecropia* may result in the death of 1000 million mealworms, and recently 1000 times more powerful killers were found. On this basis 1000 kilograms (no more than the weight of two cows) might be sufficient to kill all the insects in the world – if we could distribute the stuff in the proper way.

But even if we could achieve this, it would be an ecological disaster to destroy the whole insect world and so we need to discriminate between the 0·1 per cent that are enemies and the 99·9 per cent that are helpful or innocuous. It is like trying to kill 10,000 gangsters by spraying poison over a state like Illinois (Chicago included) or in a country like Belgium, not knowing where they live and without doing harm to the other ten million inhabitants.

Mammoths and dwarfs

As an animal's size increases, the effort needed to support and move its body also becomes greater. For this reason the largest animals are found in the sea, where buoyancy – rather than legs – provides support for their giant bodies. The heaviest creature known is the blue whale which, at a maximum of 125 tonnes, has the weight of the inhabitants of a fair-sized village (1800 people) or, in other units, of 23 full-grown elephants.

Land animals have always been more modest; the largest, the *Brachiosaurus*, living in East Africa 150 million years ago, weighed only 50 tonnes, the same as a mere 700 people. With his very long neck this creature could reach a height of 15 metres (50 feet), and if there was one living now it could easily look in at a fourth-floor window. However, this long neck would not have enabled the Brachiosaurus to walk about in deep water, because if the water were deep enough for only his head to show, the hydrostatic pressure on his body would have been one atmosphere – greater than the air pressure within his lungs – leading to unimaginable breathing difficulties.

Because it has a lower level of activity in relation to its size, a large animal gives a better yield to would-be consumers. Suppose that we had a tonne (1000 kilograms) of hay, we might use it (in rough figures):

to feed a bullock for four months, he would yield about 100 kilograms of beef; or

to feed 75 rabbits also for four months, but their yield in table-meat would be only a quarter of the bullock's.

If a mouse, with its high metabolic rate, were to eat as much as a cow does in relation to its size, it would need a stomach and digestive system three or four times larger than its body to cope with the quantity of food it would have to absorb.

Slow and fast pulses

Our pulse, usually felt in the wrist, is the number of heart-beats in a minute; for humans, 70 is the normal figure. For an elephant the rate is only 27 and for a canary it is 1000, but for all three the total time of the pauses during which the heart-muscle is resting is the same, i.e. about nine hours in the 24-hour day.

A higher pulse-rate results from quicker contractions, so that although hearts go on working day and night, the time spent in rest by the heart-muscle in any given period is about the same for any warm-blooded creature – and is, incidentally, about the same proportion of the time which in his whole lifetime a healthy human is asleep.

Much movement

The tiny creature *Paramecium caudatum*, often found in the mud at the bottom of ponds, has as many as 12,000 cilia (hairs), which are vibrating at about twenty times per second when the animal is active. To equal this in human terms, all the 2500 inhabitants of a neighbouring village would have to move each of their fingers (and thumbs) ten times a second – quite a difficult feat.

The jumping flea[21]

A human flea can jump 20 centimetres high, sixty times its own

Figure 14. If a man could jump as high as a flea in relation to its body-length, he would be able to leap over St Paul's Cathedral (110 metres, or 365 feet high).

body length. A similar feat for a man would be to jump over St Paul's Cathedral (height 110 metres, or 365 feet), which would mean jumping nearly 50 times higher than the world champion high jumper (record = 2·3 metres).

The flea's remarkable power is due to its ability to store energy in a protein called *resilin* and to release this explosively. At the moment of take-off the power produced by the animal per gram of its body weight* is forty times that achieved by man.

Consequently, as far as direct muscular force is concerned, the power output of the flea is fantastically high, but is produced only intermittently. In terms of their mean specific energy output, however, man beats the flea twice. The flea takes off very rapidly (in one millisecond) using only its hind legs, but has to keep its hind legs tucked up for about 100 milliseconds before every jump. So, in effect, it winds itself up slowly and then fires itself into the air.

Now let us compare the flea's achievements in jumping horizontally with those of man running over the Earth. The flea makes ten long jumps per second each of 30 centimetres, each one 8·5 times as long as its own body. For a man to perform a similar feat, he would have to equal the world record long jump twice every second (the record is 8·9 metres). Jumping in this way the flea travels at a speed of ten kilometres per hour. A man running at this speed, however, would have a mean specific energy output† only one-seventh of the flea. As far as the total is concerned, man's performance against the flea at running is even better than it was at high-jumping.

The walking man and the swimming duck[22]

Humans are much better at walking than ducks are at swimming! A walker may attain 15 per cent efficiency in the con-

*Flea: 20×10^6 ergs per gram per second; man: 5×10^5 ergs per gram per second.

†At 10 kilometres per hour the flea spends 17×10^{-2} kilocalorie per hour per gram, while at the same speed man spends $2{\cdot}5 \times 10^{-3}$ kilocalorie per hour per gram.

Figure 15. A swarm of locusts could contain as many as 40,000 million insects.

version of energy consumed to work done, whereas the most that a swimming duck can manage is 5 per cent. The latter figure is far worse than that of a ship, which can utilise from 20 to 30 per cent of the input energy for pushing through the water. However, we must not forget that the limitations imposed on a duck may be connected with its ability to swim, to walk on land *and* to fly through the air; no man and no vehicle can do all these.

Locusts

Locusts[23, 24] form vast, voracious swarms operating over long distances and eating, if they can find it, their own weight (two grams) of food in a day. In contrast, an adult man is satisfied with a daily intake of 0·5 kilogram of (dry) food. (He eats his own body-weight in half a year or so.)

Clouds of 40,000 million insects, weighing 80,000 tonnes, have been observed. Their potential food consumption of 80,000 tonnes on one day is equivalent to the corn necessary to feed 150 million people, two-thirds of the population of the USA, for that same day. Fortunately, it is rare that locusts achieve this potential. But it has been estimated that at least 150,000 tonnes of cereals were destroyed in Ethiopia in 1958, which would have fed the entire population for two weeks.*

Other swarms, large enough to cover 10,000 square kilometres, the area of Belgium, have been reported moving at a speed of 200 kilometres (125 miles) per day: the fastest long-distance runner would need over ten hours for this distance – if he could last the pace. And such journeys can range from Western Africa to Eastern India, with a hungry swarm flying over one-fifth of the Earth's land surface.

Cargoes from the sea

To transport all the plankton in the sea (all the small plants and animals together, estimated at 3000 million tonnes) the merchant fleet capacity of the entire world, including the tankers, would need to be increased fifteen times. For transporting all the fish in the sea (6×10^8 tonnes), a three-fold capacity of the fleet would be needed.

Penguin insulation

A female king-penguin hatches its one egg during the six months of darkness and cold in the Polar night, in temperatures as low as −40 °C; but she manages to keep the egg at +40 °C, a temperature difference of 80 °C. This is achieved in spite of biting winds in which a man unprotected by special clothing would be frozen stiff within three minutes.

Cow power

A farmer, learning that the methane produced in a cow's rumen

*In the 1971 census the population of Ethiopia was measured at 24,319,000.

can amount to 400 litres (nearly 100 gallons) in a 24-hour period[25], reasons as follows: if he could somehow collect all this gas it would enable him – even with his big American car, which does only 22½ miles to the gallon (eight kilometres per litre), to drive 1·6 miles (2·5 kilometres) every day. On the methane produced by one of his sheep in the same period (50 litres), he could travel 300 metres (328 yards).

In order to profit as much as possible from this discovery, he decides to build a barn for 20 cows, pumping the gas they produced into a small tank holding eight cubic metres (10½ cubic yards, the capacity of his automobile) mounted on a tractor. With two tractors, one being filled while the other is in use, he could cover 50 kilometres (31 miles) a day, far enough to enable him to do his daily work.

6 We human beings

The world's population on the march

The first recognisable man

At a Congress of Anthropologists held in Chicago in 1965, reports on recent finds in Tanganyika – now Tanzania – led to the conclusion that creatures recognisable as an early form of Man have existed on the Earth for 30 million years. On a rather different time-scale, studies in human embryology show that a human foetus has a recognisable form after eight weeks' development, although it only weighs one gram and is 25 millimetres (one inch) long.

A slow follow-up

A few million years before the beginning of the Christian era there lived some tribes, altogether perhaps 100,000 primitive men, whose numbers increased very slowly. Suppose for a moment that these tribes increased every year by only one single individual, which would correspond to one extra citizen per year in a town the size of Halifax, Yorkshire (or Wilmington, Delaware). If these tribes had had unimpeded growth for one million years, the number of descendants alive at the end of the period would be 2·2 thousand million, a figure actually reached on Earth about the year A.D. 1900. In view of the fact that the tribes started not one, but several million years ago, we can see that the growth rate of mankind has been considerably slower than the rate of one new mouth per year in Halifax. Whole tribes must have dwindled and perished, while only a few thrived and grew.

The acceleration of population

The world's population in about 7000 B.C. was ten million – the population of one of our largest cities, like London or Tokyo – and it took some 2500 years to double. This brings us to the time of man's earliest records, carvings on stone, which could therefore have had twenty million readers, though in fact it is probable that only a few score people were able to understand them.

From 4500 B.C. until the time of Jesus Christ four more doublings are thought to have occurred, bringing the world's population to 300 million, as many as we find now in Western Europe.

From the beginning of the Christian era, 1650 years passed before the sixth doubling took place.

The seventh doubling required only 200 years, from A.D. 1650 to 1850.

A further doubling was achieved in the following 100 years from 1850 to 1950.

In 1974 the yearly increase in the world-population amounted to two per cent, indicating that it will double in 35 years.

Every day the number of new births equals roughly the population of Plymouth, around 200,000, and by A.D. 2000 this daily number is expected to be 500,000, the population of Bristol or, in the USA, Indianapolis.

The total number of persons who have ever lived is estimated to be of the order of 100,000 million (10^{11}). This might seem an enormous crowd but in fact it is only 300 times the number of Jesus' contemporaries and 25 times our present population (4×10^9). In the last 100 years there have been more people alive on the Earth than lived in the preceding 100 centuries.

The situation today

The present birth-rate is strikingly expressed as follows:

3 babies per second
180 babies per minute

11,000 babies per hour
260,000 babies per day
90,000,000 babies per year

Thus, the world's population will soon be increasing every year by the number of people that are now living in Japan (100 million).

The bitter end[26]

The most promising way of feeding the increasing numbers of the Earth's inhabitants seems to be synthetic food production, powered by catching more of the Sun's radiation in satellite mirrors (see page 58). At present the Earth's population density is about 25 people per square kilometre. A full Earth with a population density of five million per square kilometre (that is five per square metre, standing shoulder to shoulder), would be possible if people were prepared to live in tower blocks reaching up to the stratosphere, with the upper stories pressurised like the inside of an aircraft. But if this could be achieved, why not go further? The possibility of picking up still more energy from the Sun and producing even more synthetic food does exist, but there would be one ultimate limit – the disposal of the excess heat. With over 120 million people per square kilometre – twice the population of Great Britain assembled in Kensington Gardens – the end of mankind's development on this globe would loom as the oceans gradually rose to the boil.

Man and his relatives

On page 33 we condensed the entire history of the Earth since its solidification three-and-a-half thousand million years ago ($3{\cdot}5 \times 10^9$) into the period of one calendar year, which meant that every period of ten million years was represented by about one day. In this illustration the first signs of life – bacteria – were observed in May of this compressed year and Oldowan man

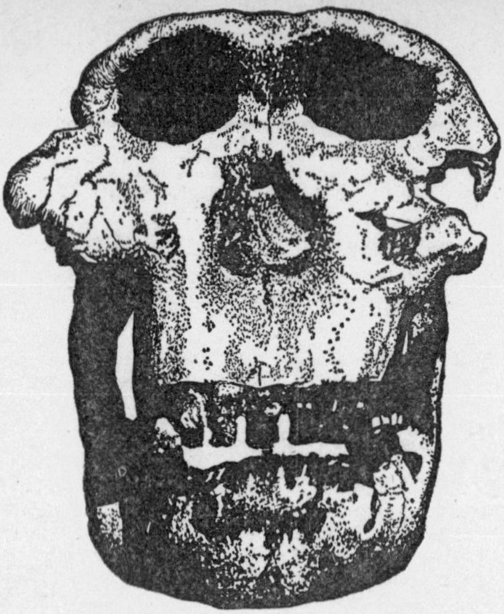

Figure 16. A drawing of the skull of Australopithecus boisei (Olduvai hominid 5), one of the earliest recognisable humans.

(Figure 16) appeared on the scene around dinnertime on the last day of the year.

But before Oldowan man appeared there was a long period of development through the ape-men or *hominids*, which eventually led to 'Man' as he is now recognised. Some indication of how these changes may have come about is provided in a study made by Butenandt on the mutations of the red colouring matter of blood[27], the *haemoglobin*. It appears that the greater the similarity in the fine molecular structure of these haemoglobins in different animals, the more they resemble each other. For example, members of all the human races – and, indeed, chimpanzees – have identical haemoglobins.

Examinations of fossil material suggests that, on the average, a mutation in haemoglobin structure can be expected once every ten million years – once a day in our concentrated time-scale. Moreover, the similarity that can still be seen between the molecules of human haemoglobins and those of the horse, the pig and the rabbit throws light on the process of evolution of these species.

On average only once in ten million years can we expect to find a mutation in the DNAs which will give rise to entirely new characteristics. This is surprising when we recall that, apart from the showers of neutrinos passing through our bodies, every-one of us is penetrated every day by about ten million high-energy particles – mostly protons – of cosmic origin, any one of which might initiate a mutation.

Man in motion

Our motor, the heart

In the industrialised countries, the usual daily cycle for most of the working population is eight hours at work, eight for meals and recreation, leaving eight for sleep. Thus one-third of the time is spent in 'rest'. The working cycle of a healthy human heart comprises 0·3 second of activity during the contraction and 0·6 second of relaxation or release, so for two-thirds of the time it is in the 'rest' condition. At first sight, this suggests that the heart is rather lazy – but it has no week-ends off and no holidays; it carries on, day and night, for seventy years or more.

The number of times your heart beats can be expressed as follows:

In one day it beats about 100,000 times, a total not far short of the population of Cambridge.

In one year it beats 36 million times, a figure equal to the population of Spain.

If you live to be eighty years old, your heart will beat 3000 million times (3×10^9), which is not far short of the present world population.

Your heart, the size of your fist, can be likened to a single-acting pump which requires 0·003 horse-power to operate it. This corresponds to the tiny electric motor that you might find in a child's toy, which yields about 2·25 watts, so with an overall efficiency of 50 per cent it requires an input of 4·5 watts. If your heart was an electric motor of this kind, it would cost less than 50p for a whole year of day-and-night service, taking the price of electricity to be 1p per kWh. In the USA it would cost $1.20 per year.

It is working hard enough to deliver heat energy at the rate of 50 kilocalories per day, nearly two per cent of the daily calorie intake of a man doing light manual work; enough energy to raise, in the course of an hour, nearly one tonne of goods (the weight of a medium-sized motor-car) from the ground to a loading platform one metre (3·3 feet) high. This energy output is proportionally eight times the average performance of the whole body, per unit of weight.

Over a lifetime of seventy years, this fist-sized power-pack pumps something like 250 million litres (55 million gallons) of blood through the body. In an industrial country a water authority has to pump – per inhabitant – only 1/150 of this quantity of water in the same seventy years, on average.

The total length of the blood vessels in an adult human body, consisting of innumerable narrow tubes, is almost 2500 kilometres (1560 miles). But the width of the greater part of this network, that of the capillary blood vessels, is only 0·009 millimetre, one-tenth the thickness of a human hair. The red corpuscles, being tiny plates with a diameter of 0·007 millimetre (and thickness of 0·002 mm), just about fit into these minute tubes with a clearance of only 0·001 mm on each side – a degree of tolerance which would arouse considerable jealousy in engineering circles. In spite of this tight fit, six litres of blood, carrying 25 million million ($2{\cdot}5 \times 10^{13}$) corpuscles, are pumped around our body each minute. However, it must be remembered that some of our blood-vessels – the main arteries, and so on – are quite large tubes, and it is also known that the circulation of blood through the lungs, for which the right side of the heart is the pump, is completed in only six seconds.

If all the blood vessels in a human body could be separated,

Figure 18. This house, 24 Energy Street, contains 24 lights of 100 watts each. The power needed to keep all of them lit continuously would be enough for *all* the owner's requirements. One light represents his daily food consumption; the four in the garage what he needs for travelling about, by rail and air as well as in his car; the remaining 19 represent all the other power that he uses in various ways. The two lights in the extension being built on the left stand for the annual increase in his power requirements.

opened and flattened out, the total area covered would be 80 square metres (96 square yards), enough material to clothe forty-five men, whose skin area would be about 1·8 square metres (nearly 2·2 square yards) each.

Our energy requirements

A person's average energy consumption of power plus food is 50,000 kilocalories per day (2·4 kilowatts), the calorific equivalent of seven kilograms (16 lb) of coal or five litres (a good gallon) of petroleum. To put it another way, it corresponds to burning 24 electric lamps each of 100 watts continuously.

One of these 24 lamps represents this man's food intake of 2000 kilocalories per day.*

*This also applies to children and people in hot climates. An adult in a moderate or cold climate doing light work consumes 2500 kcal per day.

Four lamps express the energy he uses in transporting himself about.

The other 19 lamps are the equivalent of his requirements for heating, lighting, manufacturing goods etc.

At the end of the year, two new lamps have to be added in order to keep up with his increased power needs during that year (see Fig. 18).

With a daily food intake of 2500 kilocalories, the equivalent of a handful (375 grams) of coal, two beefsteaks or – if you prefer – two teacups (250 cubic centimetres) of petroleum, man is a very efficient machine.

In supine condition he needs some 1700 kilocalories per day, so 30 per cent is available for doing work. Part of this is needed for operating his body-machinery, and one effect of this is to increase his temperature. But a final efficiency of perhaps 15 per cent can be attained, which beats the 12 per cent efficiency of a cylinder steam locomotive. One of the most strenuous jobs is chopping wood. A lumberjack might well need a daily ration of 5500 kilocalories, represented by 800 grams (1·7 lb) of coal or half a litre (just under a pint) of petroleum.

In the western countries the daily work and rest cycle is, for most of us, eight hours work and sixteen hours rest. With a five-day week, and allowing for education, holidays, illness, etc. the proportion of time that is actually spent working comes to only 15 per cent of the total. So if a man aged seventy had spent the time between his twentieth and thirty-first birthday working continuously, he would have done as much work as most men do in their entire lives, and could spend the rest of his years enjoying himself.

Feeding on alcohol

If we express the world's annual consumption of alcoholic drinks in terms of its alcohol content we come to the staggering (!) total of 7000 million litres. On the average, each of us – including non-drinkers such as Mohammedans and, we hope, children – drinks an annual two litres (about 3½ pints). Quite apart from the pleasure it gives us, this quantity of alcohol represents almost one week's calorie requirement for the world's entire population. It could also supply enough calories for the inhabitants of West Germany – 60 million of them – for a whole year. Their present consumption is above the average for, with their population about two per cent of the world's total, they drink ten per cent of the world's annual consumption of alcohol.

Faithful to their reputation, the French nation tops the list, easily beating West Germany with their average of 19 litres per person per year; in fact they derive their calorie supply for two months in every year from the alcohol in their excellent drinks. Next come the Italians, Spaniards and Portuguese all taking around twelve litres of alcohol per person per year, equivalent to their calorie-needs for some thirty-eight days. In their drinking customs the Anglo-Saxon people remain remarkably true to tradition, for in countries like USA, Canada, Australia and New Zealand, where they have emigrated in great numbers, consumption of alcohol is about the same: between five and seven litres per person per year – only a third of the Frenchman's capacity.

The housewife makes tea

When a housewife puts the kettle on to boil for her afternoon cup of tea, it takes 20 kilocalories to heat a quarter of a litre (half a pint) of cold water to just boiling. During the ten minutes or so that it takes to heat the water and to make the tea, the housewife uses up, within her body, just about the same amount of energy; this comes from her food, for while she is making the tea the nutrient elements in the food are undergoing a slow combustion.

Our bodies

Vital cycles

The average lie-span of a human cell is about 100 days, so a man disposes of one per cent of his cells each day. But this is rather a slow process compared to the rate at which fluid is replaced: half of the water in the human body is renewed within two weeks, and the turnover of red blood cells is even more rapid, half of them being replaced every seven days.

Some dental stories

The enamel

The shiny material covering our teeth consists principally of *hydroxy-apatite*, a mineral substance in the form of many tiny bars called *prismata* – of which the combined length in a cubic millimetre of enamel amounts to about 80 metres. The total volume of enamel in an adult set of teeth is estimated to be 13,000 cubic millimetres (13 cubic centimetres). Therefore the total length of the prismata is 1000 kilometres (600 miles) the distance from London to Prague. And the prismata in their turn are composed of small *crystallites*, each 4×10^{-6} centimetre long and together these would extend 10^6 kilometres, encircling the Earth twenty-five times.

Dental caries

The medical name for the enamel on teeth is *substantia adamantina* which literally means 'the imperishable'. However, 'imperishable' is not really the right word, because of the very widespread occurrence of dental caries, thought to be caused by enamel being dissolved by acids present in the mouth, the result in turn of bacterial activity.

The best known method of preventing caries is to add fluoride ions to the drinking water at the rate of only one milligram per litre: in medical terms, one part per million (1 ppm). At the age of seventy, a man might easily have drunk 50,000 litres of water (the contents of a small room), and if all this water had been 'fluoridised' it would mean that he had imbibed 50 grams of fluoride, the weight of 100 aspirin tablets. Spread out over the seventy years this would mean $1\frac{1}{2}$ aspirins every year.

The enamel on our water-drinker's teeth contains only a very small fraction of his total fluoride intake – not even 0·001 gram of fluoride – which is scarcely 1/500 of the weight of an aspirin tablet. In proportion to the 50 grams of fluoride that he drinks with water (fluoridised at 1 ppm) over his lifetime, this is in the proportion 1:50,000. This is easy to visualise, for it represents the proportion of the weight of one of his teeth to his whole body-weight.

Dental caries and used water

People who object to the contamination of drinking water by fluoridisation at 1 ppm might like to know that this is negligible in comparison with the quantity of things that we swallow with every draught. If you feel, not unreasonably, that molecules excreted in some way by a human being and then drunk by somebody else should be considered 'dirty' molecules, you might be surprised to learn the following from pages 126 and 127:

> A tiny amount of water – sufficient to fill a hollow tooth – may contain 200,000 times as many such 'dirty' molecules as there are now people on Earth (7×10^{14} 'dirties' altogether). And do you know what we inhale with each breath? Look on page 127.

Philadelphia is full of dentists

According to research conducted by the World Health Organisation, to keep our teeth really healthy we should need the services of one dentist to every thousand persons. To achieve this on a world-wide scale there would have to be as many dentists as there are citizens of Philadelphia (Pa) or Leningrad – four million.

Worms and anaemia

Hookworms are parasites of man which live in the intestinal canal, where they attach themselves to the wall to obtain their nourishment, human blood. It is estimated that one such worm can consume three cubic centimetres of blood in one day, and that one-quarter of the world's population is infected with, on the average, 100 hookworms each. If this is so, the daily quantity of blood lost by the human race to these parasites is around 260 million litres, which is twice the amount of blood used in transfusions in the USA in one year.

Body-weights

Most men weigh about 70 kilograms (154 lb) but the heaviest recorded body-weight, that of the huge American R. E. Hughes, was *seven times* as large. When he died in 1958 at the age of thirty-two, he weighed 485 kilograms (1069 lb). His coffin, a piano case, had to be lowered by a crane.

The thinnest recorded human of normal height was Miss E. Schaller, another American, who weighed only 21 kg (46 lb), thirty per cent of the average, but only four per cent of that of Hughes – about the weight of his head.

Human breezes

Sitting quietly in a chair, the average healthy man or woman breathes something like seven litres of air every minute. Breathing through our noses, as we should, and dividing the time about equally between breathing in, breathing out, and the intervening pause, we find that the 'wind speed' in the nose is two metres per second. This corresponds to a wind force of 2 on the Beaufort scale – a gentle breeze.

Doing hard physical work, the amount of air breathed in every minute increases to about 100 litres. There is now no pause between 'out' and 'in' so that the wind speed in the nose rises to about 16 metres per minute, corresponding to 7 on the Beaufort scale, a 'Strong Wind' or 'Moderate Gale'.

However, when we work hard we breathe through the mouth rather than the nose, and our wind-pipe is the 'bottleneck' of the system; the wind speed there is about 10 metres per second, 6 on the Beaufort scale or a 'Fresh Breeze', capital for sailing.

Figure 19. A sneeze can produce wind speeds as great as those in a tornado. Tornado Tracy (Minnesota, 1968), caused nine deaths and 100 injuries.

We can even find a storm indoors, for close – perhaps dangerously close – to an electric fan there will be a wind speed of 30 metres per second. This is 11 on the Beaufort scale, which indicates a Storm and there is only one higher Beaufort number – 12 – corresponding to a wind speed of 33 metres per second, which is a hurricane.

Beyond the Beaufort scale are the enormous wind-speeds generated in tornadoes, sometimes as great as 200 metres per second. You might think that this could never be found in the human body, but it is thought that a sharp cough causes air to move within the passages faster than the speed of sound, 340 metres per second.

Figure 20. The combined strength of all the hairs on this man's head would support 100 of his friends.

Just hang on

A human hair can support a weight of 80 grams, so a tubby friend weighing 80 kilograms could, as long as he is not bald, hang from 1000 of his hairs. And, if he is hung from all his hairs – about 100,000* of them – he could support 100 of his friends too, provided that his hairs were not pulled out at the roots.

Get your hair cut

A hair on your head grows nearly 20 centimetres (8 inches) each year, so that a well-covered scalp yields 200 grams (7 ounces) of hair annually. Hair from elsewhere adds another 25 per cent to this.

If we wanted to clothe ourselves with material made from our own hair, we should get no further than rather scanty underwear, for man's average consumption of textiles is about 4 kilograms (9 lb) per year, sixteen times his – or her – own crop.

*Blonde people may have as many as 150,000 hairs on their heads.

Working at a rate of one hair per second, it would take a redhead a whole day and night to cut the 90,000 hairs on his head; a person with fair hair would probably need forty hours, and the rest of us some period between these two extremes.

Left-handers

In the centuries which have elapsed since Stone-Age times, the human race has gradually become more and more right-handed. This has been attributed to the custom of carrying a shield in the left hand* and using the right for the sword or spear. Examinations of ancient tools and other archaeological discoveries have shown that:

In the Stone Age, the number of left-handed people was about equal to the number of right-handed people.

In the Bronze Age, the proportion of left-handed people had fallen to 25 per cent of the population.

Now, only about one person in every 20 is left-handed.

*Presumably to protect the heart.

7 The cultural world

Scientific developments

The explosion of science[14]

Whereas in the mid-seventeenth century there were only a few scientific men, there are now in the USA alone over a million people with scientific and technical degrees. The exponential law of doubling every fifteen years tells the simple story. And with the number of scientific journals increasing at the same rate – one journal per ten scientists has been the ratio in the past – by the year 2000 the number of journals may have passed one million, which is more than the number of scientists in the USA now.

It is most difficult to count up the number of problems being tackled by a large chemical or industrial concern in its research. Perhaps the best answer to this numerical problem – albeit not in numerical terms – was recently given by the President of the Royal Dutch/Shell Group: 'An alphabetical index of all the sciences and technologies of interest to us in our research effort would contain all the letters, from "A" for Acoustics to "Z" for Zoology'.

In Britain the percentage of the gross national product spent on research has risen:

from 1·25 per cent in 1900

to 1·60 per cent in 1954

to 2·80 per cent in 1964.

At its present rate of expansion this would equal the gross national product by the year 2020 and so we can be sure that a ceiling is in sight; otherwise the British would be unable to afford even bread.

About four per cent of the 10^{11} people who ever lived are alive now; the corresponding percentage for scientists is 80 per cent.

Simultaneous discoveries[28]

Sometimes it seems that Francis Galton's (1822–1911) remark concerning the multiplicity of discoveries was right: when apples are ripe they fall readily.

If there are 1000 apples on a tree, and 1000 blindfolded men reach up at random to pick one of them, the statistical probability is that 368 apples will not be picked at all and that 368 men will pick one apple each; the remaining 264 apples, however, will be picked by more than one person.

It is surprising to find, if we examine the records of the Patent Office, that in every 1000 discoveries about 264 of them have more than one discoverer. If we compare the probability that one apple will be picked by two or more men with the number of simultaneous scientific discoveries we find the following figures:

179 double discoveries and 184 double apple pickings.

51 triple discoveries and 61 triple apple pickings.

17 quadruple discoveries and 15 quadruple apple pickings.

Discoveries seem to be harvested like apples.

Patents: the transfer of information

At a conference on international patents in 1967, new methods of dealing with the greatly increased number of patent applications were predicted.[29] One of them results from advances in laser holography and will make it possible to transfer all the information on 100,000 standard typewritten pages to one single card the size of a car number plate. There will also be computers which can store up 100 million items of information in their memory banks and retrieve this stock within two minutes. When an inventor wishes to file a patent application in any country, an automatic call will be transmitted all over the world via satellites and the inventor will know within a few hours whether he can obtain a world patent on his idea. This is of special importance to highly industrialised countries, as is shown by the fact that in the USA the number of patents taken out is one for every 60 people, whereas in the rest of the world the average is one for every 300 people.

Going metric

In making the arrangements for the Annual General Meeting of the British Women's Tea Club, the President thought that it would be a good idea to invite a statistician to address the members on the controversial topic of metrication in relation to tea-making. Being himself a member of an international standards committee, the statistician saw nothing out of place in referring to the yearly consumption of tea in Great Britain as 4000 million litres, a remarkably large volume, amounting to 70 litres per person and which would require all of forty large tankers (100,000-tonners) to carry it.

The President, however, in her speech of thanks to the erudite lecturer courteously but firmly pointed out that in English tea clubs measurement is not yet by the litre but more usually by the pot, sometimes by the gallon, and occasionally by the 'urn', and that this would not easily be changed – 'even', she concluded 'at the insistence of your worthy committee. And,' she added, 'How is it possible to improve our familiar measure the foot, for which the standard[30] is thirty-six barleycorns taken from the middle of the ear, and which was adopted 1000 years ago when the earlier definition of four palms and sixteen fingers proved to be too variable?' She felt that the basic unit of the metric system which, she had recently read, has something to do with the wavelength of the radiation of the krypton-86 atom was unacceptable for the simple reason that in her tea club nobody had ever heard of krypton nor seen one radiation of an atom: even tea does not radiate.

Some days later the statistician returned to the subject of units in a rather different milieu, in fact at the bar. He asked his friends how they could possibly use the gallon as a measure, seeing that its relation to a decimal system is so bad that one-tenth of a gallon is equal to 454·6 cubic centimetres, a really inconvenient conversion.

A Scotsman in the party proposed the whisky-bottle as a more acceptable unit of measurement. Although its capacity of 26·6 fluid ounces is very unfamiliar on the continent of Europe, it has – particularly in respect of the contents – an established international reputation. Moreover its capacity is nearly one per cent greater than that of a standard wine bottle, 750 cubic centimetres, well known over much of the continent – especially France – so the consumer would gain a slight advantage. A further merit of the whisky-bottle as a unit of volume is that six of them make one Imperial Gallon, while five make the slightly less well-known United States Gallon; although five is half of ten, suggesting a decimal system, most customers prefer half-a-dozen for a very good reason: one more bottle!

A golfer drew attention to the facts that in this wonderful game:

the speed of the clubhead is expressed in miles per hour,

the velocity of the ball in feet per second,

the carry of the ball in yards,

and the diameter of the ball in inches.

He saw here a chance to introduce the metric system, but he was beaten by the argument that this system did not seem to be consistent with the official specification of a golf ball:

'Not heavier than 1·62 ounces'
'Not less than 1·62 inches in diameter'.

And official rules, once announced by the Royal and Ancient Golf Club at St Andrews, are not easy to alter.

A world swimming champion pointed out regretfully that under the rules of the *Fédération Internationale de Natation Amateur*, performances achieved in 50-metre and in 55-yard baths are not equivalent. The 55-yard bath is actually 11½ inches longer than a 50-metre bath – far too great a distance to be disregarded, not only because of the slight extra endurance required of the swimmer, but also because of the extreme accuracy of present-day timing devices. Our champion, who always enjoyed a visit to the continent of Europe, was therefore unable to make any attempt to better the record based on yards – his great ambition – when away from home. 'Indeed', he said, 'for my part all baths should be measured in yards and not in metres and, as far as swimming goes, you may abolish the metric system tomorrow!'

Seeing that adopting the metric system universally would lead to unexpected difficulties it was decided to leave things as they were for the time being, an upshot not unfamiliar to people used to inches and ounces.

No sooner had this decision been taken, than the current tennis champion demonstrated his agility by leaping in through an open window of the conference room. He said he was glad to hear that things were to remain as they were. 'For,' he said, 'we have in tennis a numbering system which is already accepted internationally as the method of scoring.' He went on to explain that the first 'win' scores 15 points and the second win scores the same, so two wins equal 30 points; the basis is apparently 'quinquedecimal'. However, a third win brings the score to only 40 points, so that this quinquedecimal or '15' basis has soon been lost. Our tennis champion had a logical historical explanation for this remarkable scoring system. 'It is derived,' he said, 'from the cannons in the English ships in use at the time of the battle of Harfleur, in 1415. The English victory was achieved with the help of 15-pounders, 30-pounders and 40-pounders, and it is believed that the victors celebrated their success the same evening with a game in which they used the same terminology; indeed, what could have been more appropriate?'

'So,' he continued, 'why not extend this system, which as far as tennis is concerned is already accepted all over the world, for general international use? It also brings in the useful expression 'deuce', which is derived from the French *deux encore* (in tennis, two more wins needed to win the game). So here two languages have been amalgamated, another step in the international direction.' This argument in favour of not adopting the metric system closed the meeting.

Speaking

The evolution of language

It appears that the language of a civilised culture changes slowly but steadily so that, without a dictionary, an intelligent and well-educated reader cannot expect to grasp the meaning of matter written 500 years before. This is because a modern civilised language, which may comprise up to 150,000 words, expands on average by about one word per week, and that writing is considered unintelligible when one word in four cannot be understood immediately.

Vocabularies

Western languages[31]

Shakespeare's vocabulary is estimated at 24,000 words, whereas Victor Hugo's word count contained 38,000 items. Perhaps this richer vocabulary is connected with the more advanced time in which Hugo lived, 250 years after Shakespeare (1546–1616), for a language grows with time. The ancient Greek and Roman authors living before Christ had only 3000 to 9000 words at their disposal, but don't think that this makes a poor vocabulary. The average American journalist writes his newspaper article using 6000 words, only four per cent of the arsenal of 150,000 items in a modern language. The average citizen's word count is estimated at 3000 words, only half that of the Roman masters and of the present-day journalist, but a simple farm labourer is restricted to something like 1500 words.

If the usual rate of speaking is in the region of 120 words per minute, most people could utter their daily quota of 3000 words within half an hour: in printed form it would take six pages of the book you are now reading.

The late President J. F. Kennedy, famous for his reading speed (see page 111), was also noted for the rate at which he spoke, even in public. In one of his speeches a speed of 380 words per minute was measured, which approaches the 400-words-per-minute record of the Rhodesian tobacco-auctioneers (but we hear that nobody outside the tobacco trade can understand what they are saying!).

An American discovered that the limits of one's interest are closely connected with the number of words used for building up sentences. He found the following average number of words per sentence for a person with:

Only primary education, reading cowboy books –	10
Junior high school education, reading novels –	15
Senior high School education, reading popular science books –	22
University education, reading scientific literature –	26

In the East

The Chinese alphabet comprises about 40,000 characters, each of which is an ideogram representing one specific word or idea formed or drawn to its own unique pattern. This is over 1500 times the number of letters – twenty-six – from which Victor Hugo could construct his copious vocabulary of 40,000 words, by chance the same in number as the Chinese ideographs.

To gain command of the 3000 or so words which, as we saw, are the requirement of an average citizen, the Chinese child has to learn the same number of ideograms, which may take six years, while children in the western countries using the 26-letter alphabet need only two or three years to learn the reading and writing of their 3000-word vocabulary.

A Chinese mandarin of the old type skilled in the language and usually a high Government official, could only obtain his

Figure 21. Chinese characters.

important office after ten or twenty years of study, which made him familiar with 14,000 ideograms. But even then, from the point of view of vocabulary, his knowledge was only equal to that of a western student just entering university in his eighteenth year, but the latter might have learned in the meantime three or four other languages (which is usual in several European countries; some students are familiar with as many as six languages, if Latin and Greek are included).

Animals

Scientists succeeded in 'speaking' with a chimpanzee called Sarah by means of symbols.[32] For instance when the symbol for 'banana' followed by that for 'question mark' was put on the table, Sarah would answer in a positive way by using the symbol 'give', and in a negative way by using three symbols: 'give red apple' (see Figure 22).

Sarah's vocabulary at the age of seven consisted of 120 words, nearly ten per cent of the number of words used by a simple farmer.

Incidentally, if the Chinese characters could be used for 'speaking' with animals, no new dictionaries would be required for this purpose.

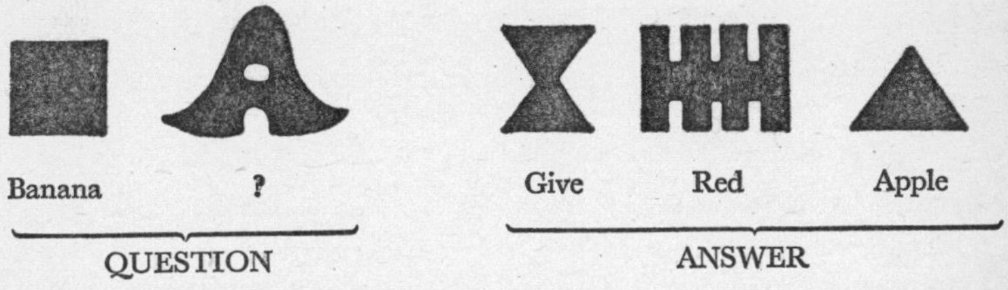

Figure 22. Talking to a chimpanzee.

Reading

Libraries past and future

In 1750, when George Washington was an adult and Napoleon

not yet born, the National Library of Paris already contained 100,000 books – which would form a row equal in length to one hour's walking distance (five kilometres, or three miles). Nowadays the row of eight million books contained in this library would stretch from London to Penzance, or from New York to Washington DC, 400 kilometres (280 miles). It has been forecast that the Library of Yale University, which doubles every sixteen years, will possess by the year 2000 a row of 200 million books, stretching from one of the poles to the Equator.

The disappointed author[28]

Every author of a scientific article hopes that his work will be read with great care and that attention will be paid to all the details he has so industriously assembled and recorded. This optimism appears to be sadly unjustified.

The largest scientific library in London is at the Science Museum and a few years ago it was reported that, of the 80,000 annual requests for journal articles, 80 per cent of them were to be found in only 10 per cent of the 9000 journals available. More than half of the current articles were not asked for at all during the year, and a quarter were asked for only once. Among the more popular journals, one was asked for on 382 occasions – the highest figure recorded – and as many as 60 articles were asked for more than 100 times.

The cynic's conclusion: 'Don't write at all; but, if you must, see that your work is accepted only in the top-ranking journals.'

High-speed reading

A substantial newspaper such as the *Daily Telegraph* may contain in one issue 100,000 words, excluding what is printed as advertisements. This is about the same number of words as in a 200-page novel.

To read all these words successively, the overall length of the lines of print scanned by the eye would be at least a kilometre in length (0·6 mile). Since for a normal reader 250 words a minute (15,000 per hour) is a usual speed, the time to read all the articles in the daily paper is 6½ hours with the eye running along the lines at a speed of 150 metres per hour. So 33 hours of reading involves seeing a line of print as long as the distance covered in one hour's walking (five kilometres).

Four hours a day is as much as most people spend reading, and in this time, at the same linear speed, the reader would scan some 600 metres (660 yards) of print. Many of us, however, need to read much more than this and so are forced to use a 'vertical' reading technique. It is known that the late President J. F. Kennedy could work through four newspapers within 20 minutes; if his reading had been 'horizontal' – that is, if he had read each successive word – his point of vision would have had to move at 12 kilometres per hour (7 m.p.h.), the speed of an unhurried cyclist, but eighty times the speed for a 'horizontal' reader.

A blind person, running a finger-tip along the line of tiny impressions which constitute Braille script, needs an hour to cover the 3000 words that most of us use in a day.

The alphabet in space

The number of ways in which the twenty-six letters of our alphabet can be arranged – that is, the number of possible permutations – is $1 \times 2 \times 3 \times \ldots \times 25 \times 26$ usually written '26!' and amounting to just over 4×10^{26}.

Suppose that all these arrangements are written out on ordinary paper 25 cm × 20 cm (10 in × 8 in), and 0·08 mm (about 0·003 in) thick, with thirty arrangements on each sheet. For the total number of permutations we should need 5×10^{10} cubic kilometres of paper, enough to cover the surface of the Earth with a layer reaching up to the height where falling meteorites begin to glow and the 'Northern Lights' have their origin, 100 kilometres (60 miles) above the Earth's surface.

If, instead, we were to write out our arrangements of the alphabet on a long continuous strip of paper, we should need a piece 160 million light-years long, that is 2000 times the diameter of the galaxy in which our Sun and solar system lie and which we see as the 'Milky Way'.

Figure 23. Reading Braille.

Some cultural achievements

Creating a horse

The Koran says that Allah created horses out of the south-west wind that blows across the desert. A pedantic student named Abdullah set himself to calculate how much wind would have been needed, assuming the law of conservation of mass. He found in his textbook that the mass of one cubic metre (1·3 cubic yards) of air at the Earth's surface is 1·26 kilograms (2·8 lb), so he worked out that 400 cubic metres (500 cubic yards) of it would be needed for a horse of 500 kilograms (1100 lb). This would be all the air contained in the mausoleum (7 m × 7 m × 8 m) of a high-ranking Muslim like the ones Abdullah found in many churchyards.

By contrast, the heart – even of a pedigree racehorse – needs

Figure 24. The air in this Muslim mausoleum could, assuming conservation of mass, be compressed to make a horse (copied from a rock painting in the Sahara).

only five cubic metres ($6\frac{1}{2}$ cubic yards) of air, the quantity set free when a Bedouin takes down his small travelling tent.

Idiot or savant?[33]

In 1940 twins were born in the USA, and by the time they were twenty-four they displayed such a mixture of alternating brilliance and stupidity that they earned the description of 'idiot savants'. Charles and George cannot add, subtract, multiply or divide simple single-digit numbers, but their self-taught calendar calculations go beyond anything reported hitherto.

Although Charles is completely accurate only for this century, George can project his calendar calculations over the range of our civilisation (6000 years). For example, he can instantaneously identify February 15, 2002 as a Friday, or August 28, 1591 as a Wednesday. When asked in what years April 21, the birthday of one of their friends, fell on a Sunday, both will promptly answer 1968, 1957, 1953, 1946 and so on.

Rock-and-roll noise

Industrial and military experts get worried about exposing people for long periods to a noise level above 85 decibels*, which is somewhere between the roar from a train passing over a bridge just above our heads and the exhaust crackle of a powerful motorcyle a few feet away.

Recently 125 db have been recorded at rock-and-roll concerts, which is only 15 db short of a jet plane at 30 yards and which is described as 'the threshold of pain!' Airport ground staff wear ear protectors at this noise level and so it is not surprising that 25 per cent of the freshmen at Tennessee University, would-be pop musicians, had measurable hearing losses and that some had already deteriorated to the 65-year-old hearing level.

*A decibel (db) is the unit in which sound levels are compared. The lower unit of audibility for a good ear corresponds to an intensity of about 10^{-6} watt per square centimetre, often taken as one decibel.

Long-playing records

A conscientious conductor, preparing for his orchestra's Festival season, decided to let the 100 players run through *all* the works of various classical masters, to help him in making up the Festival programme. Realising that this would be a long job, he persuaded the players to perform for twelve hours each day. After thirty-six days, of which twenty-eight were for Mozart and eight for Beethoven – still not having made up his mind – he saw that Bach would need fifty-six more days and Haydn another sixty, bringing the total playing time up to nearly six months. Meanwhile, the kettle-drummer, who had always been good at physics, was able to calculate[31] that the energy of the sound

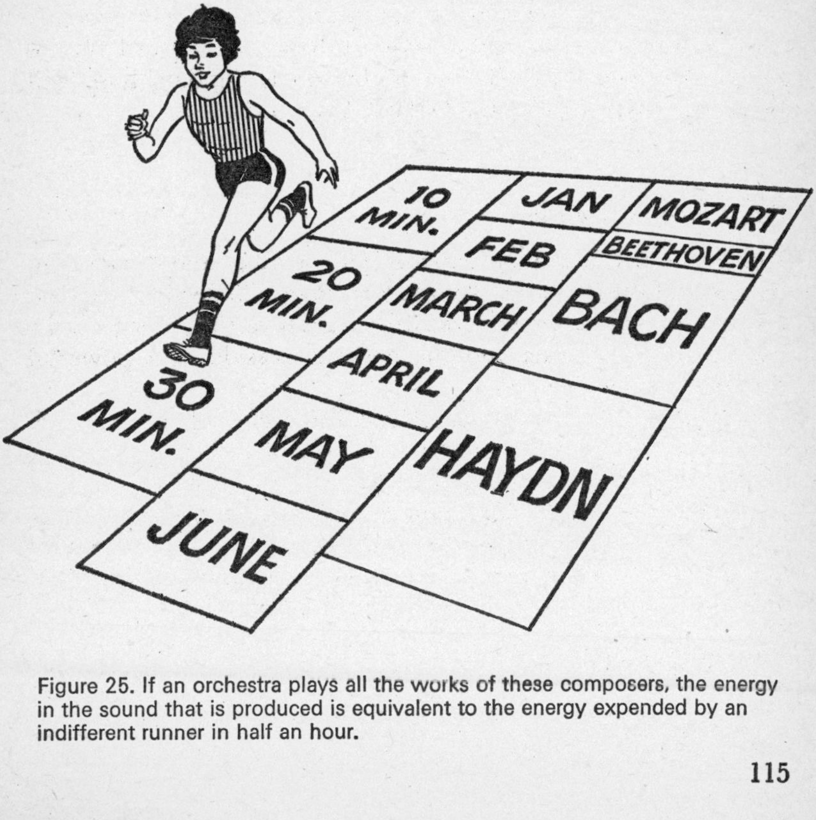

Figure 25. If an orchestra plays all the works of these composers, the energy in the sound that is produced is equivalent to the energy expended by an indifferent runner in half an hour.

produced in this performance (approximately 0·5 kWh) would be comparable to the energy used by a typical runner in half an hour. Faced with this discouraging news, the orchestra at first refused to play any more, but after some discussion they gave Richard Wagner's works a run-through which, surprisingly, took only another two days.

9 Polluting our own environment[34, 35]

Air pollution

Of the real necessities of life, air to breathe is obviously one of the most important to man, and in the short-term it is the most important of all. While he can live for two weeks without food, and for two days without water, he would be dead in a few minutes without air. Each day approximately 130 times our body volume* of air (about ten cubic metres) circulates through an adult's lungs.

The main pollutants in the atmosphere are carbon compounds, particularly carbon dioxide (CO_2) and carbon monoxide (CO), but nitric oxide (NO) and sulphur dioxide (SO_2) are being added to these older-established contaminants at an increasing rate. Perhaps this is the right place to remind those who complain about the pollution of the atmosphere by industry that in the USA less than 20 per cent of the whole discharge comes from factories; 60 per cent comes from traffic in various forms, and most of us contribute to this very high proportion in one way or another.

Carbon dioxide (CO_2)

Before the Industrial Revolution the CO_2 content of the air was 280 parts per million (ppm) by volume or 415 ppm by weight, and this level was more or less constant. Then the increase started, leading to this overall picture:

The CO_2 content of the atmosphere at present is 322 ppm (by

*The average body-weight of an adult is 70 kilograms (volume 70 litres).

Figure 26. Air pollution from industrial sources represents only 20 per cent of the total – most of it comes from traffic.

volume) representing $2 \cdot 2 \times 10^{12}$ tonnes, 11,000 times the weight of all living people.*

Each year an additional 1·4 ppm is generated, resulting in 8×10^9 tonnes – forty times the weight of that crowd. Fortunately, half of it is absorbed in some form by the biosphere and the oceans, but the other half is added to the air, thus increasing its CO_2 content by 0·7 ppm (or 0·2 per cent) per annum.

Mankind contributes 15 per cent of this annual total simply by exhaling. This amounts to 300 kilograms (660 lb) each, so by the end of a year each person has breathed six times his own bodyweight into the air in the form of carbon dioxide.

Carbon monoxide (CO)

Carbon monoxide is a dangerous poison because of its affinity for haemoglobin in the blood, which takes up oxygen and distributes it throughout the body, bringing back carbon dioxide which is then exhaled. The affinity of carbon monoxide for haemoglobin is 250 times greater than that of oxygen, so oxygen molecules have less chance of finding a haemoglobin particle and unconsciousness or death can follow. There is at least 500 times more carbon dioxide than carbon monoxide in the atmosphere; if these proportions were reversed we should all be poisoned, for 300 ppm by volume would be just enough for observable chronic poisoning. Here are some figures showing the permitted levels of carbon monoxide in the air:

In many countries workers must not be exposed to more than 0·005 per cent (50 ppm).

In busy streets a level of 0·01 per cent (100 ppm) is considered dangerous; in a few countries the limit is 50 ppm.

Discomfort and even sickness can occasionally occur at 0·02 per cent (200 ppm).

The lower limit for chronic poisoning is 0·03 per cent (300 ppm).

*4×10^9 people, weighing (including children) 50 kilograms each, adding up to 2×10^8 tonnes.

Death will occur within a few hours if the concentration reaches 0·3 per cent (3000 ppm).

There is no doubt that our industrial requirements have greatly increased the importance of carbon monoxide and 200 million tonnes of it are now produced each year – the weight of everyone now living, but still only 2·5 per cent of the carbon dioxide that is produced. Fortunately, carbon monoxide does not stay in the air indefinitely – the time is estimated at between 0·1 and 4 years. There is evidence that certain soil constituents act as a sink[40] where anaerobic bacteria oxidise it to carbon dioxide. The absorbing capacity of the continent of the USA alone is estimated at three times the world-wide carbon monoxide production from all human activities.

In what follows we shall describe the quantity of carbon monoxide needed to produce the 300 ppm limit in a man's daily air intake as the *maximum daily dose* of carbon monoxide. In fact, this amounts to the contents of three vermouth bottles full of carbon monoxide, containing one litre (1·76 pints) each, in the volume of air that could be contained in a small (15-seater) motor-bus (ten cubic metres). The weight of this carbon monoxide is about the same as a couple of the teeth (four grams) of a two-year-old boy weighing 13 kilograms – the weight of the air contained in the bus.

Since a human body[36] produces 15 cubic centimetres of carbon monoxide per day, mainly by breathing, one person would have to spend 200 days in the bus to produce enough poison to fill the three bottles. However, after five days he would have produced 500 litres of carbon dioxide and it is easy to calculate that all the oxygen in the bus would have been consumed by then. So there is no danger of poisoning yourself with your own carbon monoxide in a closed room.

But this also means that anyone who in the course of some activity – be it smoking, driving his car, or anything else – produces three litres of carbon monoxide, has made enough to contaminate a day's supply of air for one of his fellow men (or, for that matter, for himself), to the extent of causing chronic carbon monoxide poisoning. In the USA the annual discharge

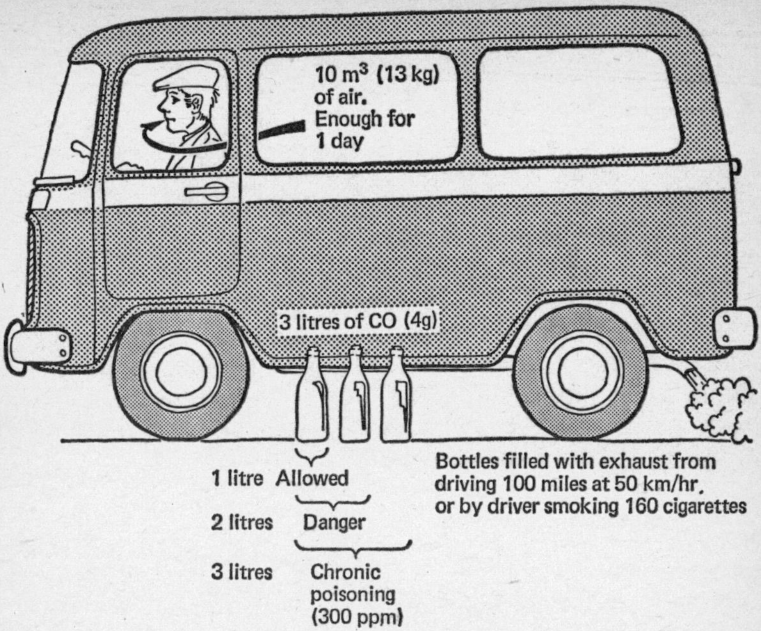

Figure 27. This minibus contains ten cubic metres of air, the volume that you might breathe in a day. The bottles each hold a litre of carbon monoxide, and emptying three of them into the bus would make a lethal mixture. The bottles could be filled from the exhaust of the bus, or by the driver smoking 160 cigarettes.

into the air is 75 million tonnes of carbon monoxide, half of the total waste of the nation. This is enough to supply the maximum permitted daily dose of carbon monoxide to every American for a period of 250 days – roughly the number of working days in a year – if there were no rapid conversion by bacteria and no natural circulation of the air above the country.

Fear has also been expressed that the oxygen content of the atmosphere is being reduced because of the increasing use of fossil fuels (five per cent per year). However, even if all the estimated fossil reserves were burned up only five per cent of the available oxygen would be converted.

Poisoned by traffic

Throughout the world there are now over 200 million passenger cars in use plus 50 million commercial vehicles. A passenger car produces annually some 1000 kilograms (2200 lb) of harmful gases, the weight of a medium-sized car itself. Amongst these gases are 700 kilograms of carbon monoxide (the weight of a small car), 100 kilograms of hydrocarbons (the weight of a very fat passenger) and 35 kilograms of nitric oxide (the weight of a ten-year-old boy).

As we drive our car into town at 50 kilometres per hour (about 30 m.p.h.), every 100 metres (110 yards) one maximum daily dose of carbon monoxide (300 ppm) is emitted for one of the passers-by. And, when we find ourselves in a traffic-jam, crawling along at only 15 kilometres per hour (just under ten m.p.h.), this contamination can be trebled, so that the lethal dose for one bystander is produced every 35 metres (40 yards). Actual measurements show that at a busy street-crossing in a city, the air near the pavement – which is breathed by the public – is continually at or near the chronic poisoning concentration of carbon monoxide.

In New York alone, street traffic produces 4000 tonnes of this gas every day. The result could be a layer of contaminated air as high as a house (10 metres, or 33 feet) over the whole area of the city. Although the population of New York City is estimated at 14 million, there is enough carbon monoxide discharged to provide eighty daily doses for each citizen every single day: so it is fortunate that a great deal of New York's air is blown out to sea!

If we could smell carbon monoxide

Traffic in Los Angeles discharges over 10,000 tonnes of carbon monoxide into the air every day. There are 300 million tonnes of air to dilute this contaminant but, even so, the average concentration in the city's streets is 370 ppm, well above the limit for chronic poisoning. If the exhaust gases from road vehicles included fatty acids – like those found in man's perspiration – on the same scale as carbon monoxide, then the situation would be quite intolerable in any town or city with substantial motor traffic. We can smell these fatty acids when they are present in a proportion of only one in a thousand million, i.e. 1/370,000 of Los Angeles' carbon monoxide concentration. In these circumstances, complaints about (motor) body-odour could only be avoided by reducing the number of vehicles 1/370,000 of the present figure, leaving only a few score machines to carry people about.

SOS – Save Our Smokers

Cigarette smoke is very poisonous, with its 20,000 ppm (two per cent) or more of carbon monoxide, which is nearly seventy times more than the lower limit for chronic poisoning (300 ppm). One cigarette produces 0·02 gram of carbon monoxide, twice the weight of the cigarette paper. Fortunately, even those who inhale draw only a small proportion of this into their lungs, where the concentration of carbon monoxide may reach 400 ppm: this is still well above the 300 ppm limit, so a chain-smoker suffers continuously from this degree of poisoning.

If all the carbon monoxide produced in one year by smoking tobacco could be collected and liquefied, it would load a 65,000-tonne tanker, which is enough to poison everyone's daily air-intake five times over. The two packets a day smoker produces ninety 'maximum daily doses' of 300 ppm in the course of a year.

Smoking a packet of cigarettes a day means inhaling 6×10^{-7} gram of benzpyrene, but a non-smoker living in Detroit inhales 1·3 times this amount every day, and a Londoner inhales fives times this amount.

Anyone who is still alive after fifty years of smoking two packets (forty cigarettes) per day, has consumed in tobacco and paper the weight of a prize bull (900 kilograms, or 2000 lb). At the same time he has produced a quantity of smoke equal to the weight of the pig which took first prize at the same show (370 kilograms, or 830 lb).

Aerosols[37]

One cubic centimetre of smoke from a non-filter cigarette usually contains about 5×10^9 particles of dust, tar, etc., which means just over one particle for each of us. The densest aerosol that has so far been reported gives only 10^5 particles per cubic centimetre, one for each of the inhabitants of a town the size of Cambridge. The weight of all the particles dispersed into the atmosphere, $1{\cdot}6 \times 10^9$ tonnes per year, is eight times the weight of carbon monoxide generated. A man living in a metropolis and sharing the dust in the air above his city with a million others, inhales during his lifetime (seventy years) a quantity of dust (50 grams) equal in weight to a three- to four-centimetres-deep layer all over his scalp. A farmer in a rural district inhales just enough to cover his scalp with tiny hairs 0·5 centimetres long.

Traffic versus smoking

We have seen that one man's daily dose of carbon monoxide (300 ppm) can be produced by a car driven at 50 kilometres per hour (30 m.p.h.) over a distance of only 100 metres (110 yards), or by smoking 160 cigarettes. Smokers may be pleased to hear that although the world's annual consumption of cigarettes is estimated at three million (3×10^{12}), the amount of carbon monoxide produced from smoking could be equalled by the motor-car population in one of the smaller countries, like Greece, with 130,000 passenger cars, if each one was driven as little as 15,000 kilometres (9000 miles) per year at an average speed of 50 kilometres per hour (30 m.p.h.). But anyone who inhales the smoke from his cigarette should not complain that he is being poisoned by traffic, because the concentration of carbon monoxide in his lungs (400 ppm) is greater than that in Los Angeles (360 ppm) – known as the 'city of smog'.

'Man,' said a public health expert, 'is the messiest of beasts. The best cure for air pollution is to hold one's breath and to park one's car!'

Water pollution

Man pollutes his water supply in all sorts of ways; we shall consider two of the worst cases.

Oil

We spill some two million tonnes of oil per year – 0·1 per cent of our total production – into the waters, mainly from oil tankers and refineries. It has been estimated[35] that if we add the fall-out of airborne hydrocarbons on to the surface of the sea, the amount contaminating the oceans at present may approach 0·5 per cent of the production. It could just be transported by the Russian tanker fleet – or, if you prefer, it weighs as much as the entire population of the USA. The sinking of just one of the modern mammoth tankers could add more than one per cent to the amount of petroleum entering the ocean in one single year.

In 1969 the oil layer on the oceans was estimated as being three molecules thick. If it ever became ten molecules thick, it would seriously hamper the capacity to absorb carbon dioxide of which the oceans are an important reservoir.

Oil globules and tar balls have been found to be more abundant in the Sargasso Sea (part of the Atlantic) than the *Sargassum* weed from which the sea is named.

DDT

DDT* though its use is now being phased out in many Western countries, is still being used elsewhere in the world on a large scale as a pesticide and this has given rise to ecological surprises since the discovery of its toxic properties by a Nobel Laureate. It enters the sea either through rivers or from dispersal by the air, and of the two the latter is the main route for transfer. The accumulated world production of DDT is estimated at 2×10^6 tonnes, with an annual production of 10^5 tonnes, a quarter of which (the load capacity of a small tanker) reaches the sea.

In the calculations behind these figures the precipitation over the oceans is estimated to contain 80 parts per 10^{12}: this is as if

* *D*ichloro *D*iphenyl *T*richloroethane.

there was just one murderer in thirty times the Earth's population.

The 3000 million tonnes of plankton in the sea already contain 0·01 parts per million (ppm) of DDT. The 600 million tonnes of fish that depend on plankton for their food supply has concentrated this figure by a factor of 100 up to 1 ppm and 5 ppm is the limit allowed in our food. So we are a fifth of the way to being poisoned when we eat fish. But in certain countries, the permitted limit is only 1 ppm: if you drank a litre of milk per day that was contaminated up to that limit, you would be consuming three times the maximum safe quantity. The cargo of the small tanker mentioned earlier, 25,000 tonnes of DDT, which reaches the seas every year is sufficient to contaminate seventy times the whole world population up to the limit proposed by the World Health Organisation (5 pp 10^9 on the body-weight) – if all the DDT released were actually absorbed by us.

Second-hand molecules

Inspector Veryfit of the Public Health Department was having a drink with his old friend Dr Pure, who was in charge of the Waterworks. Veryfit was worried. 'I have an uncomfortable feeling,' he said, 'that sometimes I am drinking water that has been drunk before.' Dr Pure consulted his note-book and replied that things looked very bad indeed; the total number of people ever to have lived he estimated at a hundred thousand million (10^{11}), and their average lifespan was only twenty-five years (– the infant mortality rate was high until very recently). If all these people excreted two litres of water every day of their lives, roughly one molecule in every million has been excreted by someone at some time. 'Assuming', Dr Pure added, 'that all the water on the Earth is thoroughly mixed up.'

'So the number of "dirty" molecules in your glass of beer, my dear Veryfit, is in the region of 15 million million million – far more than you can imagine. To give you some idea of the numbers involved, think of the cavity in a hollow tooth: it could contain 10^{20} molecules, which means more than 10^{14} "dirty" ones – 200,000 molecules each for everyone now living.

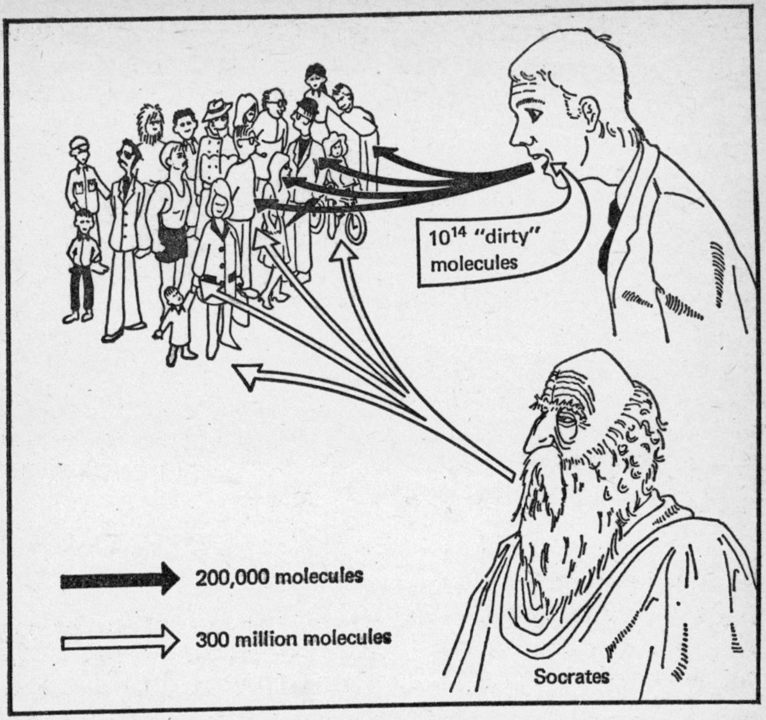

Figure 28. A cavity in your tooth might hold 10^{20} water molecules of which 10^{14} have been excreted by somebody in the past. With every breath you inhale 300 million molecules that have been previously inhaled by some particular person – Socrates, for instance.

Number of molecules in one cubic centimetre of water	$= 3{\cdot}4 \times 10^{22}$
Number of molecules in one litre of air	$= 2{\cdot}7 \times 10^{22}$
Volume of water on and around the Earth	$= 1{\cdot}3 \times 10^{21}$ litres
Volume of air around the Earth	$= 4{\cdot}0 \times 10^{21}$ litres

'Of course,' he went on, 'some of these molecules have been excreted *more than once*, so there are "double-dirty" ones; and on top of that, the "dirty" water is *not* distributed evenly over the Earth and it is likely to be much dirtier in densely-populated areas like this.'

The Inspector poured his beer down the sink, calculating that if there was one 'dirty' molecule per million there would be enough in his pint to provide every living person with a hundred million of them! A young scientist had been listening to this conversation from behind his newspaper, but this waste of beer prompted him to point out to Inspector Veryfit that the concentration of dirty molecules was really very low – the same, for instance, as the amount of fluoride added to the water to prevent tooth decay. 'In the air you breathe,' he continued, 'about one molecule in every 500 has been exhaled by someone else: this is 2000 times the concentration of the dirty molecules in the Inspector's beer.

'And in every breath you inhale about half a litre of air, or 10^{22} molecules, so about 300 million of these molecules have previously been exhaled by some *particular* person who lived to the age of forty – Socrates, Shakespeare or Einstein, for example. Isn't it rather wonderful to think that we are breathing the same air as these people?'

'Another round!' said Inspector Veryfit, encouraged by these inspiring words, 'but nothing for Dr Pure, who has made no attempt to size up his knowledge!'

Noise pollution

The human ear is a remarkably sensitive organ,[31] for the lower limit of audibility is an intensity of 10^{-16} watts per square centimetre, which is called a *decibel* (db).* Under ideal conditions of sound-propagation (no conversion to thermal energy, absence of wind) we might hear in Rome a 100-watt sound source installed at the North Cape, Norway (or in Miami one installed at Montreal), 3000 kilometres (1900 miles) away.

The ear can also survive without damage short-lived surges of sound 10^{14} times as high as the lower threshold mentioned. Fortunately, the loudness of a sound does not increase proportionately with the stimulus: when we increase the sound

*See footnote on page 114.

power ten times, we only double the sensation of loudness: otherwise a clap of thunder might deafen us.

But we must also consider people's comfort, and the limits are measured by the level of noise that is acceptable without interfering with concentration or performance and, at the upper end of the scale, the level that is actually dangerous to health[38]. Most people would soon begin to feel annoyed by the continuous noise in even a relatively quiet city street (about 55 PNdB*); heavier traffic, and the occasional screech of brakes, can reach a level of 85 PNdB, which is almost the safety limit for long exposure.

Most noise pollution is from road and air traffic – industrial noise is much more localised. The streets in many cities are already noisier than the tolerable level, but heavy lorries can produce 70 PNdB, and small motor-cycles give out a continuous 80 PNdB, sometimes as much as 110 PNdB. This is comparable to the staccato pounding of a pneumatic drill across the street and is far beyond the damage risk limit.

The power generated by an airliner as sound can be as much as 50 horse power (37 kilowatts), enough to run a car or, expressed in calories, enough food for 300 grown-ups during the flying time (100 kilocalories per person per hour). The take-off and landing produce particularly disturbing noise-levels (100–120 PNdB). It has been suggested[39] that we should establish a proper financial balance between the economic gain which a neighbourhood derives from the existence of an airport and the loss of local amenities and investments (the depression of the prices of houses and other properties in these areas because of the noise nuisance). But this would obviously not solve the noise problem itself and it seems reasonable that the passengers who enjoy the benefits of air travel should pay their share in the form of higher fares, if the money were used to reduce the exit velocity of the jets or to add suppressor nozzles. Reducing the noise to a reasonable level might involve an increase in fares of about 20 per cent. On a trip from New York to London this would mean paying an extra £20 or so ($35).

* *P*erceived *N*oise level in *deciB*els.

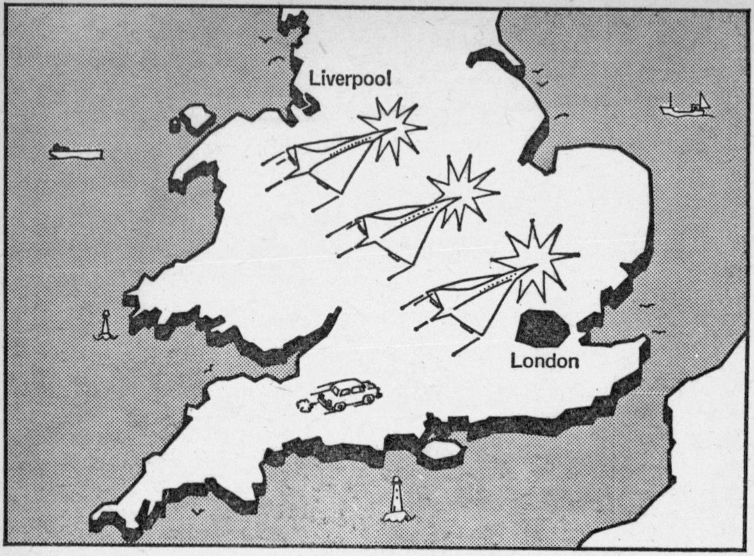

Figure 29. Three jets could wake up the people between London and Liverpool with their sonic booms. The power radiated as sound by an airliner would be enough to operate a motor-car.

A problem of a completely different character is the *sonic boom* which can form a sort of carpet 50 to 130 kilometres (30 to 80 miles) wide, trailing like a stream behind the aircraft. If this carpet is 100 kilometres wide three or four jets, flying parallel and producing their booms simultaneously, could act as alarm-clocks to wake up people in London and Liverpool at the same moment: fifty jets could do the same for New York and San Francisco.

An occasional boom, causing a pressure-change of no more than 7×10^{-4} atmosphere, would be quite acceptable to the general public and booms of 10^{-3} atmosphere (a pressure change of 0·1 per cent over the atmospheric pressure) cause no damage to buildings. But because of atmospheric conditions once in every 1000 'acceptable' booms there occurs one 'super-boom', exceeding 2×10^{-3} atmosphere and this *can* cause substantial damage to buildings.

Basic numerical data

Length

1 km = 1094 yd = 1000 m = 0·6214 mile
1 m = 1·09 yd = 100 cm = 39·37 in = 3·28 ft
1 cm = 10 mm = $10^4\,\mu$ = 10^8 Å

1 mile = 5280 ft = 1760 yd = 1609 m = 1·61 km
1 yd = 3 ft = 0·914 m = $9{\cdot}14\times10^{-4}$ km = $5{\cdot}68\times10^{-4}$ mile
1 in = 2·54 cm = 0·083 ft

1 light second = $3{\cdot}00\times10^5$ km = $1{\cdot}86\times10^5$ mile
1 light year = $9{\cdot}46\times10^{12}$ km = $5{\cdot}88\times10^{12}$ mile

Area

1 km^2 = $1{\cdot}20\times10^6$ yd^2 = 10^6 m^2 = $2{\cdot}47\times10^2$ acre = 100 ha = 0·39 $mile^2$
1 m^2 = 10^4 cm^2 = $1{\cdot}55\times10^3$ in^2 = 10·76 ft^2 = 1·196 yd^2

1 $mile^2$ = $3{\cdot}10\times10^6$ yd^2 = $2{\cdot}59\times10^6$ m^2 = $6{\cdot}40\times10^2$ acre = 259 ha = 2·59 km
1 yd^2 = 8354 cm^2 = $1{\cdot}30\times10^3$ in^2 = 9 ft^2 = 084 m^2
1 in^2 = 6·45 cm^2 = $6{\cdot}94\times10^{-3}$ ft^2 = $7{\cdot}71\times10^{-4}$ yd^2 = $6{\cdot}5\times10^{-4}$ m^2

Volume

1 km^3 = $1{\cdot}31\times10^9$ yd^3 = 10^9 m^3 = 10^{12} l
1 m^3 = 1000 l = 220 gal = 35·3 ft^3
1 l = 1000 cm^3 = 61 in^3 = 1·76 pint = 0·22 gal = 0·035 ft^3

1 $mile^3$ = $5{\cdot}45\times10^9$ yd^3 = $4{\cdot}17\times10^9$ m^3 = 4·17 km^3
1 yd^3 = 765 l = 168 gal = 27 ft^3
1 pt = 34·6 in^3 = 0·568 l
1 in^3 = 16·38 cm^3 = $1{\cdot}6\times10^{-2}$ l = $3{\cdot}61\times10^{-3}$ gal = $5{\cdot}79\times10^{-4}$ ft^3

Mass
1 lb = 0·4536 kg = 453·6 g
1 ton = 2240 lb = 1016 kg = 1·016 tonne

Time
1 h = 60 min = $3{\cdot}6 \times 10^3$ s
1 day = 24 h = 1440 min = $8{\cdot}64 \times 10^4$ s
1 year = $8{\cdot}77 \times 10^3$ h = $5{\cdot}26 \times 10^5$ min = $3{\cdot}16 \times 10^7$ s

Temperature
T °C = 0·556 (T °F − 32)
T °F = 1·8 T °C+32
T K = T °C+273 = 0·556 (T °F+459·67)
Absolute zero = O°K = −273° C

Velocity

Light in vacuum	= $2{\cdot}998 \times 10^5$ km s^{-1} = $1{\cdot}079 \times 10^9$ km h^{-1}
Sound in air (at 15 °C)	= 340 m s^{-1} = 1224 km h^{-1}
Brownian motion (H_2)	= 2 km s^{-1} = 7200 km h^{-1}
Electron in orbit	= $2{\cdot}2 \times 10^3$ km s^{-1} = 8×10^6 km h^{-1}

Energy
1 kilocalorie (kcal) = $1{\cdot}16 \times 10^{-3}$ kilowatt hours (Whk)
= $4{\cdot}66 \times 10^{-11}$ gram mass equivalent
= 3·97 British thermal units (Btu)
= $4{\cdot}19 \times 10^3$ joules (J)
= $4{\cdot}85 \times 10^{-8}$ megawatt days (MWd)
= $2{\cdot}62 \times 10^{22}$ electron volts (eV)
= 427 kilogram metres (kg m)
= $3{\cdot}09 \times 10^3$ foot pounds force (ft lbf)
= $4{\cdot}19 \times 10^{10}$ ergs (erg)

Power
1 kilocalorie per second (kcal s^{-1}) = 4·19 kW
= 3·97 Btu s^{-1}
= $2{\cdot}61 \times 10^{22}$ eV s^{-1}
= 5·62 horse power (hp)
= 427 kg m s^{-1}
= $3{\cdot}09 \times 10^3$ ft lbf s^{-1}
= $4{\cdot}19 \times 10^{10}$ erg s^{-1}

Energy equivalents

	kcal	kWh	kg m
1 kg standard coal	7 700	9·0	$3{\cdot}3 \times 10^6$
1 kg crude oil	11 800	12·8	$4{\cdot}7 \times 10^6$
1 m^3 natural gas	9 800	11·4	$4{\cdot}2 \times 10^6$
1 kg trinitrotoluene (TNT)	1 000*	1·1	$4{\cdot}2 \times 10^5$
1 kg oil or fat (nutritional value)	9 800	11·4	$4{\cdot}2 \times 10^6$
1 kg protein (nutritional value)	4 500	5·2	$1{\cdot}9 \times 10^6$
1 kg carbohydrate (nutritional value)	4 000	4·6	$1{\cdot}7 \times 10^6$

1 kg of matter, according to the Einstein equation ($E = mc^2$)
$= 3{\cdot}1 \times 10^7$ kg of coal
$= 2{\cdot}5 \times 10^8$ kWh

Atoms

Mass, charge of nucleons etc., see Table 2 (page 21)
Mass of hydrogen atom $= 1{\cdot}674 \times 10^{-24}$ g

Molecules

Avogadro Constant (number of atoms in one mole) $= 6{\cdot}023 \times 10^{23}$
Number of molecules in 1 cm^3 of water $= 3{\cdot}3 \times 10^{22}$

The Universe

Diameter of the observable universe $= 4 \times 10^{22}$ km
$= 4{\cdot}2 \times 10^9$ light years

The Sun

Diameter $= 1{\cdot}4 \times 10^6$ km $= 0{\cdot}87 \times 10^6$ miles
Surface $= 6{\cdot}2 \times 10^{12}$ km^2 $= 2{\cdot}4 \times 10^{12}$ miles^2
Volume $= 1{\cdot}42 \times 10^{18}$ km^3 $= 3{\cdot}41 \times 10^{17}$ miles^3
Density $= 1{\cdot}41$ g cm^{-3}
Mass $= 2 \times 10^{30}$ kg
Energy emitted $= 9{\cdot}26 \times 10^{22}$ kcal s^{-1} $= 3{\cdot}86 \times 10^{23}$ kW

* Depending on the quality. Figures range between 700 and 1100 kcal kg^{-1}.

The Earth

Diameter (equatorial) = $1{\cdot}28 \times 10^4$ km = $7{\cdot}9 \times 10^3$ miles
Surface = $5{\cdot}1 \times 10^8$ km^2 = $1{\cdot}97 \times 10^8$ miles^2
Volume = 10^{12} km^3 = $2{\cdot}4 \times 10^{11}$ miles^3
Density = $5{\cdot}52$ g cm^{-3}
Mass = $5{\cdot}97 \times 10^{24}$ kg
Gravitational constant (G) = $6{\cdot}67 \times 10^{-8}$ dyn cm^2 g^{-2}
= $6{\cdot}67 \times 10^{11}$ Nm^2 kg^{-2}
Acceleration of gravity (g) = $9{\cdot}81$ m s^{-2} (Brussels)
Total power intercepted from the sun = $4{\cdot}12 \times 10^{13}$ kcal s^{-1}
= $1{\cdot}73 \times 10^{14}$ kW
Useful power intercepted from the sun = $2{\cdot}88 \times 10^{12}$ kcal s^{-1}
= $1{\cdot}21 \times 10^{14}$ kW

The Moon

Diameter = $3{\cdot}48 \times 10^3$ km = $2{\cdot}16 \times 10^3$ miles
Surface = $3{\cdot}8 \times 10^7$ km^2 = $1{\cdot}5 \times 10^7$ miles^2
Volume = $2{\cdot}20 \times 10^{10}$ km^3 = $5{\cdot}27 \times 10^9$ miles^3
Density = $3{\cdot}33$ g cm^{-3}
Mass = $7{\cdot}33 \times 10^{22}$ kg

Bibliography

General sources

The Guinness Book of Records (Guinness Superlatives, London, 1972)
Basic Statistics of the European Communities (Brussels, 1971)
The *1972 World Almanac* (Doubleday and Co, New York)
J. G. Stark and H. G. Wallace, *Chemistry Data Book* (John Murray, London, 1970)

References

1. For books dealing with similar studies see:
   R. Houwink, *The Odd Book of Data* (Elsevier, New York, 1965)
   R. Houwink, *Data, Mirrors of Science* (Elsevier, New York, 1970)
2. J. H. de Boer, *The dynamical character of adsorption* (The Clarendon Press, Oxford, 1968)
3. M. J. Marples, *Scientific American*, Jan. 1969, p. 108
4. A. B. Cambel, *Science Journal*, Oct. 1967, p. 57
5. M. King Hubbart, *Scientific American*, Sept. 1971, p. 61
6. *Time*, 11 March, 1966, p. 50
7. F. Hoyle. *The Nature of the Universe* (Penguin Books, Harmondsworth, 1963)
8. R. C. Tolman, *Relativity, Thermodynamics and Cosmology* (Oxford, 1946)
9. Tj. de Vries, *Prisma*, No. 1231, Utrecht, 1967, p. 28
10. E. Glaser, *J. of Microwave Power*, Dec. 1970, p. 211
11. E. Stuhlinger, ibid, p. 207
12. E. Justi, *Bild der Wissenschaft*, Jan. 1967, p. 21
13. A. B. and M. P. Meinel, *Physics Today*, Feb. 1972, p. 44
14. C. Zener, *Physics Today*, 1973, p. 48
15. *The Guinness Book of Animal Facts and Feats* (Guinness Superlatives, London, 1972)
16. H. L. Penman, *Science Journal*, May 1968, p. 43
17. *Umschau in Wissenschaft und Technik*, Nov. 1968, p. 336
18. J. A. Gulland, *Science Journal*, May 1968, p. 81

19. I. Asimov, *Life and Energy* (Bantam, New York, 1965)
20. J. Postgate, *Microbes and Man* (Penguin Books, Harmondsworth, 1969)
21. H. C. Bennet Clark, *New Scientist*, 7 Sept. 1967, p. 484
22. *New Scientist*, 16 April 1970, p. 104
23. J. Hillany, *New Scientist*, 12 Oct. 1967, p. 98
24. W. von Braun, *New Scientist*, 11 Dec. 1969, p. 546
25. T. C. Byerly, *Science*, 25 Aug. 1967, p. 890
26. J. H. Fremlin, *New Scientist*, 29 Oct. 1964
27. A. Butenandt, *Deutsche Apotheker Ztg*, 2 Jan. 1969, p. 1
28. D. J. de Solla Price, *Little Science, Great Science* (Columbia Univ. Press, 1963)
29. *Science Journal*, Aug. 1967, p. 21
30. Lord Richie Calder, *Scientific American*, July 1970, p. 17
31. Modified and extended from R. Houwink, *Data, Mirrors of Science* (Elsevier, New York, 1970)
32. D. Premack, *Naturwiss. Rundschau*, March 1971, p. 118
33. *Scientific American*, Aug. 1965, p. 46
34. J. Rose, *Technological Injury* (London 1969)
35. *Man's Impact on the Global Environment* (M.I.T. Press, Cambridge, Mass, 1970)
36. J. R. Goldsmith and S. A. Landaw, *Science*, 20 Dec. 1968, p. 1352
37. F. Wheeler, *New Scientist*, 1 Oct. 1970, p. 10
38. J. M. Rodda, in J. Rose, *Technological Injury*, London 1969, p. 165
39. E. Richards, *New Scientist*, 24 Sept. 1970, p. 622
40. R. E. Imman, c.s., *Science*, 1971, p. 1229

Index

More Beaver Books

We hope you have enjoyed this Beaver Book. Here are some of the other titles:

Why Does a Glow-worm Glow? A Beaver original. Dozens of answers to intriguing questions on science topics, illustrated throughout by Mike Jackson and with a lively text by Professor Eric Laithwaite, well known as a contributor to the BBC radio programme *Dial-a-Scientist*

The Beaver Book of Brain Ticklers A Beaver original. Intriguing puzzles and teasers of a mathematical type invented by Charles Booth-Jones; illustrated with cartoons, diagrams and line drawings

Looking at Wildlife A Beaver original. Nicholas Hammond has written an invaluable guide for young naturalists, with lots of information on all kinds of wild creatures as well as advice on the best ways of observing them. Illustrated throughout

The Pool of Fire The last book of John Christopher's 'Tripods' trilogy which brings to a dramatic climax the story of the struggle to overthrow the Masters, invaders from outer space. The first two books are *The White Mountains* and *The City of Gold and Lead*, both published in Beavers

They Amazed the World A Beaver original. A collection of stories about all kinds of people whose achievements have amazed the world, from Nelson to Florence Nightingale and Einstein to Edison; fully illustrated, for readers of nine upwards

New Beavers are published every month and if you would like the *Beaver Bulletin* – which gives all the details – please send a stamped addressed envelope to:

Beaver Bulletin
The Hamlyn Group
Astronaut House
Feltham
Middlesex TW14 9AR

382117